Understanding Heaven's Court System

Understanding Heaven's Court System

Explosive Life Changing Secrets

Bill Vincent

Understanding Heaven's Court System

Copyright © 2016. All rights reserved.

No part of this publication may be reproduced, stored in a retrieval system or transmitted in any way by any means, electronic, mechanical, photocopy, recording or otherwise, without the prior permission of the author except as provided by USA copyright law.

All scripture quotations, unless otherwise specified, are taken from the [King James Version].

The opinions expressed by the author are not necessarily those of Revival Waves of Glory Books & Publishing.

Published by Revival Waves of Glory Books & Publishing
PO Box 596 | Litchfield, Illinois 62056 USA
www.revivalwavesofgloryministries.com

Revival Waves of Glory Books & Publishing is committed to excellence in the publishing industry.

Book design Copyright © 2016 by Revival Waves of Glory Books & Publishing. All rights reserved.

Published in the United States of America

Paperback: 978-1-68411-122-0

Hardcover: 978-1-68411-123-7

Table of Contents

Introduction vii

Chapter One: Reclaiming Authority 1

Chapter Two: The Commanding Power of God 7

Chapter Three: God Will Command His
Blessings to Come Upon Us 37

Chapter Four: Court System of Heaven 45

Chapter Five: Prophetic Decrees 71

Chapter Six: Prophetic Decrees Have Power 97

Chapter Seven: Break All the Way Through 117

Chapter Eight: Reassignments Coming 129

About the Author 135

Recommended Books 137

Introduction

After writing nearly fifty books and being in the ministry for over twenty-five years; this book is one of the most shocking revelations I have ever received. I'm not just saying that. God took me through a series of sermons on authority, commanding Heaven's Court and prophetic decrees. I mean to tell you that there were things from the '90s that were totally removed from my memory of understanding. There were many brand-new things that I had never even heard before. After the unction of the Holy Spirit to first teach it, then He spoke to write on these things.

This book has the potential to change your life forever if you take hold of it. This book is for all walks of life who have found Jesus as their personal savior. I really do hope you enjoy this book and I pray that it ministers to you as it has my family and those who have attended Revival Waves of Glory Ministries in Raymond, IL.

Chapter One

Reclaiming Authority

At this time, God is causing a new breed of Saints that will find their new level of authority. Jesus paid the price so we can walk in the same authority that Jesus did in the flesh. The church seems to forget that Jesus not only died but also was resurrected by the power of the Holy Spirit. I believe we are still supposed to have that power. Do you believe that? If you're reading this, I assume you do. I really believe that we need to re-attain the authority that was given in the Garden of Eden. Because of what Jesus did, we have that right to everything that Adam and Eve destroyed and lost. The devil succeeded in stealing their dominion. The whole church lost their dominion that the devil succeeded to take.

There're a lot of beautiful people gathering together on Sunday mornings, a lot of people are gathering together singing songs, hearing a word, and then going home. The next week, they do it again. People you know, people I know; people you love, people I love. The problem is they're living in a day of fallen Adam and Eve, not a day of a resurrected Jesus Christ. Religion is not what God is coming back for. He is returning for a glorious church.

Recently, Tabitha was running errands and I had a lot of private time, when all of a sudden, I heard God say this, "Many within the church love Me, but many within the church don't know Me. It's become a charade."

It's become nothing more than going through the motions. People have been playing church. As a church, we have gotten away from the true Gospel, the true power of God. I'm telling you - God has gotten left out of the church. Everybody's going around with that good old-time religion. "Give me that old-time religion" is an old song we used to sing. We say we want God to move but our actions say something else. You know what that song really should mean, and I believe it might have when it was originally written before it was put in a hymnal give me that old-time religion back in the book of Acts. That's what religion was supposed to be. Turning the world upside down. Religion has become dead instead of alive. How can the Church expect anything from the Lord when it is dead old religion?

To make matters worse, the disobedience of Adam and Eve caused all of humanity, all of us to suffer under one curse of sin to lose our dominion on the earth. Much hasn't changed; one man's decision can be a downfall for a whole lot of men and women. Sometimes you don't realize that your decisions are critical until it's too late. Do you know Adam and Eve probably didn't realize what they were carrying upon their shoulders? This time we can talk bad about it and can even refer to their story as a fallen Adam and Eve…

This time we can talk ill about it and can even refer to their story as fallen Adam and Eve….

We can mock it, talk about it, refer to it, but you know what – until you get to the place… Until you are put in that place, until you get to the place where you are put in a paradise and told not to partake of one part, one fruit, you cannot ever say, "I wouldn't touch it." We all would probably do the same thing. Christians sin or make huge mistakes, sinning every day. Since Jesus paid the price for our sin and took it all upon himself; we are much like Adam falling over and over again.

There are ministries that I have been around, ministers that tell me I will never have an affair. A lot of times you know what, the reason is that they never had a chance. I never had ostrich but nobody has offered it to me either. It is easy to say we won't sin when the opportunity has never come our way. Sometimes, we get to the place we think of ourselves higher and above everyone else, yet we have never been put in their place, put in their shoes.

I believe what I'm doing right now is saying we need to redeem ourselves as a Body of Christ for Heavenly Court to come back in session. We cannot have heavens court backing us if we are walking in the fallen Adams and Eves shoes. We all lost power to make kingly decrees, but God did not leave us helpless. God is moving upon us to reclaim our authority.

He sent Jesus Christ. He sent Jesus Christ to rescue us. He gave us his living word to come boldly before the Throne of Grace to participate in a Divine Court System. We are able to do that because of what Jesus did for us. God has given us a better dominion than in the beginning. Even with what Adam and Eve did, we have a better dominion than they had. Our dominion includes a spiritual dominion where we can take authority over the devil in the heavenly realm. We can take authority over everything that the devil tempts us with. You need to take authority over the devil in the heavenly places. Sometimes, you have to battle through. This is called heaven. Earth is heaven. Doesn't seem like any heaven to me. Biblically, it's considered a heaven. Where the devil is and all his cohorts are in is the second heaven. This is our temporary residence because they have a judgment where they're going to spend eternity in hell except for the demons that have already been cast to the dry places. There's a third heaven where God is and all the angels and the supernatural throne zone.

I pray that the presence of God invades your life right now where you are. A lot of times, when you're pressing in and you're not really feeling the glorious presence of God, it's because you're having to battle through that second heaven to get to the third heaven.

A lot of the body of Christ has given up and we have gotten complacent to where we're not battling through anymore. This is not what God is sending His Son back for. I'm telling you the violent need to take it by force. We've got to stop allowing the enemy to distract us and push us back. The enemy will keep us bound if you let him.

We have a God-given right to call forth heaven to come down. We do! We have the right to participate in that courtroom in heaven, where the devil accuses, and God and his angels carry out justice.

The devil accuses from his heaven and God releases justice from His heaven. Let me tell you something when you line up to heaven's court, God's court, everything in heaven always overrides Satan's plans. It's a guaranteed court system if you do it right. In the rest of this book, you will find a new level that will truly change everything you have ever known about authority and the power of God.

Understanding Heaven's Court System

Chapter Two

The Commanding Power of God

I had a moment of time in my life in July 2016 where I thought I was losing my mind. I was at a new place in God and I felt lost. Everything was brand new like I had never experienced in my life. I was feeling like I couldn't remember common day to day things. It lasted for weeks.

Joshua 10:13, 14 (KJV)

13 And the sun stood still, and the moon stayed until the people had avenged themselves upon their enemies. Is not this written in the book of Jasher? So the sun stood still in the midst of heaven, and hasted not to go down about a whole day.

14 And there was no day like that before it or after it, **that the Lord hearkened unto the voice of a man***: for the Lord fought for Israel.*

Understanding Heaven's Court System

Sometimes, there are experiences that happen in the things of God that once they happen, they never happen again. It is because nobody else can find that same place to make it happen. Nobody seems to be able to find that level of anointing.

Isaiah 45:11 (KJV)

*11 Thus saith the Lord, the Holy One of Israel, and his Maker, Ask me of things to come concerning my sons, and concerning the work of my hands **command ye me**.*

Our authority releases God's Power. When we are abiding in God, we are able to tap into commanding power. God wants to move in your life. Especially if we have received prophecies about something, we are able to command the power of God. Sometimes, God is waiting for us to come in agreement with Him and when we command his hands, we are coming in agreement with him.

There are a number of keys to seeing the miraculous power of God manifest when praying the commanding prayer or when you command his hands. God wants to move in power through His people more than you could ever imagine. One of the least understood, and therefore seldom practiced, is the fact that healing and even miracles are under the authority of the believer.

God has already provided His healing power and placed it on the inside of every born-again believer. I could refer to 1 Peter 2:24 concerning healing but it is more than that revelation that *by His stripes we were healed*. When talking about healing power, it is up to us to release it. Understanding and using our authority is the key to seeing miracles happen. It is time that any sick among us are able to receive healing.

Look at how Peter and John ministered healing to the lame man in Acts 3:1-8.

Acts 3:1-8 (KJV)

3 Now Peter and John went up together into the temple at the hour of prayer, being the ninth hour.

2 And a certain man lame from his mother's womb was carried, whom they laid daily at the gate of the temple which is called Beautiful, to ask alms of them that entered into the temple;

3 Who seeing Peter and John about to go into the temple asked an alms.

4 And Peter, fastening his eyes upon him with John, said, Look on us.

5 And he gave heed unto them, expecting to receive something of them.

Understanding Heaven's Court System

6 Then Peter said, Silver and gold have I none; but **such as I have I give thee: In the name of Jesus Christ of Nazareth rise up and walk.**

7 And he took him by the right hand, and lifted him up: and immediately his feet and ankle bones received strength.

8 And he leaping up stood, and walked, and entered with them into the temple, walking, and leaping, and praising God.

When God speaks to me through the revelation of His Word, I notice clues in the Word that God brings to life. Notice that Peter didn't pray for this man. He also didn't ask God to heal him. He said, "Such as I have I give thee." This didn't mean that Peter was the source of this healing. Notice what Peter said in Acts 3:12.

Acts 3:12 (KJV)

12 And when Peter saw it, he answered unto the people, Ye men of Israel, why marvel ye at this? or **why look ye so earnestly on us, as though by our own power or holiness we had made this man to walk?**

It was God's power that healed this man but that power was under Peter's authority. Peter went on to say in verse 16 that it was faith in the name of Jesus that had wrought this miracle.

Acts 3:16 (KJV)

16 And his name through faith in his name hath made this man strong, whom ye see and know: yea, the faith which is by him hath given him this perfect soundness in the presence of you all.

Peter didn't ask God to heal this man. Today, the church begs God to do something that God has already paid for. Peter believed the Lord had already done His part and had placed that power within him. Now it was Peter's responsibility to release that power and that's just what he did. Anyone who takes ahold of this can see the power of God move.

The Lord never told us to pray for the sick in the sense that we ask Him to heal them. He told us to *heal the sick, raise the dead, cleanse the lepers and cast out devils*. There is a big difference between the two. It has to do with operating in the authority He has already given us. It is time for the power of God like we all have never seen before. Look at these commands the Lord gave His disciples.

Understanding Heaven's Court System

Luke 9:1-2 (KJV)

Then he called his twelve disciples together, and gave them power and authority over all devils, and to cure diseases.

2 And he sent them to preach the kingdom of God, and to heal the sick.

Matthew 10:1 (KJV)

10 And when he had called unto him his twelve disciples, he gave them power against unclean spirits, to cast them out, and to heal all manner of sickness and all manner of disease. "And as ye go, preach, saying, The kingdom of heaven is at hand. Heal the sick, cleanse the lepers, raise the dead, cast out devils: freely ye have received, freely give."

Matthew 10:7-8 (KJV)

7 And as ye go, preach, saying, The kingdom of heaven is at hand.

8 Heal the sick, cleanse the lepers, raise the dead, cast out devils: freely ye have received, freely give.

Jesus told us to heal the sick not pray for the sick. What a major statement! This will get you kicked out of most churches today but these are the exact words of our Lord Jesus Christ. Critics can't argue this because of what Bill Vincent says because it is what Jesus Christ says. This is precisely why more people don't see the miraculous results they're praying for. We need to know who we are and who our God is. They aren't taking their authority and commanding God's power; they're passively asking God to do what He told them to do. I know this goes contrary to popular Christian doctrine. Religion has made the church sick and weak. We're constantly told that it's not us but God who is the healer and I agree with that totally. This is the truth but there is more. I also believe that God has placed His healing power under our authority and it is up to us to release it. If we don't take our authority and become commanders instead of beggars, God's power will not be released. We are co-laborers with God not just servants of God. There needs to be a radical renewing of our thinking on this issue.

If people are able to take hold of this revelation, many will be healed in many ways. This is exactly what happened with the early church. Peter had people lined up in the streets so that if only his shadow would touch them, they would be healed.

Understanding Heaven's Court System

Acts 5:15 (KJV)

15 Insomuch that they brought forth the sick into the streets, and laid them on beds and couches, that at the least the shadow of Peter passing by might overshadow some of them.

Isaiah 45:11 (KJV)

11 Thus saith the Lord, the Holy One of Israel, and his Maker, Ask me of things to come concerning my sons, and concerning the work of my hands command ye me.

What a powerful scripture! What does the Lord mean when He tells us to command Him? This is where religion and relationship seem to divide. Well, He definitely doesn't mean we are mightier and more powerful than Him and can order Him around. He means, concerning the things He has already done, He wants us to take our authority and command His power. We have the ability, by God, to get things done. It's like electricity. The power company generates power and delivers it to your house. It's not your power but it's under your control. You don't call the power company and ask them to turn the lights on. No! They won't do that. They generate the power but it's under your command. You simply flip the switch on the wall and command the power to work. Does this mean you are the power source? Certainly not! You aren't the power source but you are the one in control of what that power does. You can plead with the power company all you want, but they won't flip the switch for you. You have to assume your authority and acknowledge the power is under ***your command***. That's what the Lord was speaking of. God has already supplied healing through Jesus Christ. He did it over two thousand years ago when He bore our stripes on His back. Then He placed His resurrection power inside every believer.

Ephesians 1:19-20 (KJV)

19 And what is the exceeding greatness of his power to us-ward who believe, according to the working of his mighty power,

20 Which he wrought in Christ, when he raised him from the dead, and set him at his own right hand in the heavenly places.

He's done His part and now it is up to us to do ours. We need to take the authority He has given us and become commanders instead of beggars. This is a powerful truth that works and it's the reason we see so many miraculous healings. We have seen cancers healed, people get out of wheelchairs, blind see and deaf hear. We aren't just praying for the sick; we are healing them in Jesus' name.

We are not done here. This all literally means that men have the authority to pray in such faith that they can direct the Almighty to do for them those things which they want and need.

God would rather do things for His people than to withhold from them. To command, God is an expression of the highest relationship, friendship, and co-operation with God. God doesn't want us to be lacking anything.

It is a rare privilege to command Him and if exercised properly in a fervent petition, there is nothing that will be impossible to the believer. That is what God had intended for Adam and Eve. Also, this kind of authority and relationship with God was restored with Jesus' resurrection and restoration.

Examples of commanding God:

Exodus 8: 3 (KJV)

And the river shall bring forth frogs abundantly, which shall go up and come into thine house, and into thy bedchamber, and upon thy bed, and into the house of thy servants, and upon thy people, and into thine ovens, and into thy kneading troughs:

Exodus 8:31 (KJV)

And the LORD *did according to the word of Moses; and he removed the swarms of flies from Pharaoh, from his servants, and from his people; there remained not one.*

Exodus 32:12-14 (KJV)

¹² Wherefore should the Egyptians speak, and say, For mischief did he bring them out, to slay them in the mountains, and to consume them from the face of the earth? Turn from thy fierce wrath, and repent of this evil against thy people.

¹³ Remember Abraham, Isaac, and Israel, thy servants, to whom thou swarest by thine own self, and saidst unto them, I will multiply your seed as the stars of heaven, and all this land that I have spoken of will I give unto your seed, and they shall inherit it forever.

¹⁴ And the LORD *repented of the evil which he thought to do unto his people.*

Joshua 10:12 (KJV)

12 Then spake Joshua to the Lord in the day when the Lord delivered up the Amorites before the children of Israel, and he said in the sight of Israel, Sun, stand thou still upon Gibeon; and thou, Moon, in the valley of Ajalon.

Understanding Heaven's Court System

1 Kings 18:36-38 (KJV)

36 And it came to pass at the time of the offering of the evening sacrifice, that Elijah the prophet came near, and said, Lord God of Abraham, Isaac, and of Israel, let it be known this day that thou art God in Israel, and that I am thy servant, and that I have done all these things at thy word.

37 Hear me, O Lord, hear me, that this people may know that thou art the Lord God, and that thou hast turned their heart back again.

38 Then the fire of the Lord fell, and consumed the burnt sacrifice, and the wood, and the stones, and the dust, and licked up the water that was in the trench.

2 Kings 1:10-12 (KJV)

10 And Elijah answered and said to the captain of fifty, If I be a man of God, then let fire come down from heaven, and consume thee and thy fifty. And there came down fire from heaven, and consumed him and his fifty.

11 Again also he sent unto him another captain of fifty with his fifty. And he answered and said unto him, O man of God, thus hath the king said, Come down quickly.

12 And Elijah answered and said unto them, If I be a man of God, let fire come down from heaven, and consume thee and thy fifty. And the fire of God came down from heaven, and consumed him and his fifty.

Luke 4:35 (KJV)

35 And Jesus rebuked him, saying, Hold thy peace, and come out of him. And when the devil had thrown him in the midst, he came out of him, and hurt him not.

Acts 3:6 (KJV)

6 Then Peter said, Silver and gold have I none; but such as I have give I thee: In the name of Jesus Christ of Nazareth rise up and walk.

Acts 5:16 (KJV)

16 There came also a multitude out of the cities round about unto Jerusalem, bringing sick folks, and them which were vexed with unclean spirits: and they were healed every one.

Acts 9:34 (KJV)

34 And Peter said unto him, Aeneas, Jesus Christ maketh thee whole: arise, and make thy bed. And he arose immediately.

Understanding Heaven's Court System

Acts 9:40 (KJV)

40 But Peter put them all forth, and kneeled down, and prayed; and turning him to the body said, Tabitha, arise. And she opened her eyes: and when she saw Peter, she sat up.

Acts 13:11 (KJV)

11 And now, behold, the hand of the Lord is upon thee, and thou shalt be blind, not seeing the sun for a season. And immediately there fell on him a mist and a darkness; and he went about seeking some to lead him by the hand.

Acts 14:10 (KJV)

10 Said with a loud voice, Stand upright on thy feet. And he leaped and walked.

Acts 19:11-12 (KJV)

11 And God wrought special miracles by the hands of Paul:

12 So that from his body were brought unto the sick handkerchiefs or aprons, and the diseases departed from them, and the evil spirits went out of them.]

In the Word of God, there is much revelation on prayer that moves God yet few people notice or offer up such utterance. What is it? It is "authoritative prayer". There are many forms of prayer that we all should know including the prayer of praise, prayer of thanksgiving, prayer of asking, and prayer of intercession but we know very little of prayer of authority. Authoritative prayer is that which occupies a most significant place in the Word. It signifies authority even the command of authority.

Now, if we desire to be men and women of prayer, we must learn this authoritative kind. It is the type of prayer which the Lord refers to in Matthew 18:18.

Matthew 18:18 (KJV)

18 Verily I say unto you, Whatsoever ye shall bind on earth shall be bound in heaven: and whatsoever ye shall loose on earth shall be loosed in heaven.

Here is loosing prayer as well as binding prayer. The movement of heaven follows the movement of the earth. Heaven listens to the words on earth and acts on the earth's command. Whatsoever is bound on earth shall be bound in heaven, and whatsoever is loosed on earth shall be loosed in heaven. It is not an asking or begging on earth but a binding on earth; it is not an asking on earth but a loosing on earth. And this is an authoritative prayer.

Understanding Heaven's Court System

"Command ye me." How do we dare to command God? Is this not too absurd? Too audacious? But this is what God himself says. Undoubtedly, we should not in the least allow the flesh to come in here. However, we are hereby shown that there is a kind of commanding prayer. According to God's view, we may command Him. Such utterance needs to be learned specifically by all of us.

We find some revelation looking at Exodus 14. When Moses led the children of Israel out of Egypt, he came to the shore of the Red Sea. A serious problem arose. Before them was the Red Sea and behind them were the pursuing Egyptians. At that moment, the Israelites were truly in a predicament. They saw the Egyptians coming after them and they were afraid. They cried to the Lord on the one hand and murmured against Moses on the other. How did Moses react? From the word of God, we learn that Moses cried to the Lord. But then God told him:

Exodus 14:15-16 (KJV)

15 And the Lord said unto Moses, Wherefore criest thou unto me? speak unto the children of Israel, that they go forward:

16 But lift thou up thy rod, and stretch out thine hand over the sea, and divide it: and the children of Israel shall go on dry ground through the midst of the sea.

The rod which God gave to Moses represents authority. God even asked, *"What is in your hand?"* to Moses. So that what God meant by His words was you do not need to cry to Me, you may use authoritative prayer; you pray the prayer of commanding and I will do the work. Therefore, what Moses learned and experienced here was authoritative prayer or the prayer of command.

Isaiah 45:9-13 (KJV)

9 Woe unto him that striveth with his Maker! Let the potsherd strive with the potsherds of the earth. Shall the clay say to him that fashioneth it, What makest thou? or thy work, He hath no hands?

10 Woe unto him that saith unto his father, What begettest thou? or to the woman, What hast thou brought forth?

11 Thus saith the Lord, the Holy One of Israel, and his Maker, Ask me of things to come concerning my sons, and concerning the work of my hands command ye me.

12 I have made the earth, and created man upon it: I, even my hands, have stretched out the heavens, and all their host have I commanded.

13 I have raised him up in righteousness, and I will direct all his ways: he shall build my city, and he shall let go my captives, not for price nor reward, saith the Lord of hosts.

Understanding Heaven's Court System

God's overcomers must learn how to use the authority of Christ and pray authoritative prayers. Prayer in the scriptures is not only an asking but even more so an expression of authority. Command with authority is authoritative prayer. Therefore, God's overcomers must, on the one hand, be faithful in denying their own selves, the world, and Satan; but on the other hand, know how to exercise the authority of Christ.

We should let God defeat us with the cross so that we may be defeated before God. God is to be our source for everything. We are to defeat Satan by using the authority of Christ so that we may win the victory over Satan. Authoritative prayer is not begging, it is commanding; for there are two kinds of prayer: not only the prayer of requesting but also the prayer of command:

Isaiah 45:11 (KJV)

[11] Thus saith the LORD, the Holy One of Israel, and his Maker, Ask me of things to come concerning my sons, and concerning the work of my hands command ye me.

Commanding prayer begins at the ascension of Christ. The death and resurrection of Christ, as we have seen, so that His death concludes all that is in Adam, His resurrection gives us new ground and

His ascension makes us sit in the heavenly places far above all rule and authority and power and dominion and every name that is named: not only in this world but also in that which is to come. We are to be sitting with Christ in heavenly places. As Christ is far above all rule and authority, so we also are above all rule and authority. Scripture tells us that the position of Christ is in the heavenly places. We also should know that our place in Christ is sitting with Him in the heavenly places.

Regular prayer is praying from earth to heaven. Commanding prayer is a prayer from heaven to earth. The prayer in Matthew 6 is petitionary prayer and therefore is upward in direction. The prayer in Ephesians 6 is commanding prayer and so it is downward. We sit in the heavenly places and pour forth commanding prayer. "So be it" or "So it is". These are commanding prayers. At the beginning of any warfare, Satan tries to unseat us from our heavenly position which is one of victory. Warfare is a battle for position. Therefore, victory lies in occupying the right place. Being in Christ and sitting in heavenly places alone gives an authoritative prayer.

Simply put, "Say unto this mountain" that is, it is commanding the mountain. It is not speaking to God. It is an authoritative prayer. It is not asking God to deal with the mountain, the latter of which represents things that hinder us. Only with perfect faith can we speak to the mountain. Now perfect faith comes out of perfect knowledge of God's will. We command what God has already commanded; we decide on that which God has already decided. Due to the fact of fully knowing God's will, such faith as this is possible.

He who sits on the throne is God the Lord. He who succumbs beneath the throne is the enemy. Prayer links us with God. All who overcome and reign as kings know how to pray. We are to be heavenly representatives who know how to exercise the authority of God's throne. For the overcomers to rule over the church, the world, and even the powers of the air, they must rely on the authority of the throne.

Spiritual warfare is offensive as well as defensive. The control is not only over the nations but also over Hell and its principalities, authorities, powers, and dominions. We need to use the authority of Christ because all things are subject under His feet since He is the head of the church. If we use the authority of God, we may bring all things under our feet too.

Matthew 18:18-19 (KJV)

18 Verily I say unto you, Whatsoever ye shall bind on earth shall be bound in heaven: and whatsoever ye shall loose on earth shall be loosed in heaven.

> *19 Again I say unto you, That if two of you shall agree on earth as touching any thing that they shall ask, it shall be done for them of my Father which is in heaven.*

This commanding prayer has facets about it. Bind all the disturbances to the work that comes from people of the world; bind all the evil spirits and demons; and bind Satan and all his activities. We are to rule as kings over all things. Whenever a thing happens in the world or among the Body of Christ that is the moment for us to rule as kings. Loosing, we may also lose people. Loose all those that are timid; loose all who ought to come out and work for the Lord; loose money in the grip of people that it might be given for God's use; and loose the truths of God. We are ambassadors of God and therefore we enjoy extraterritoriality on earth. We may call in heaven to rule over the earth.

I am confident "command ye" is not a question but confident of God's will because that will is entirely known upon a problem. Certain aspects of your words help in this proof, when you said, "We do not know" or "Not sure" or "Big trouble" and the kicker, "Cease to be the Sovereign God". These quotes of yours speak of doubt and instability and confusion and Satan eats that stuff up. What I see you doing is taking confidence away from brothers and sisters which is unhealthy. But where God has stipulated something in no uncertain terms there His will may be commanded back upon Him according

Understanding Heaven's Court System

to His righteousness for He abides not only in His promises but all that is of Himself. Truly, Satan wants to cast doubt upon our hearts. Don't let him win.

When I was working a sales job, we learned that most people have to hear something seven times before we hear and understand something. Let's spend some more time concerning Command Ye Me.

Isaiah 45:11 (KJV)

11 Thus saith the Lord, the Holy One of Israel, and his Maker, Ask me of things to come concerning my sons, and concerning the work of my hands command ye me.

Mostly, we do not command God but secondarily we do. When we command a thing in obedience to Him, like the disciples commanded healings, deliverances, provisions and miracles, it is God who performs them.

Mark 11:23 (KJV)

23 For verily I say unto you, That whosoever shall say unto this mountain, Be thou removed, and be thou cast into the sea; and shall not doubt in his heart, but shall believe that those things which he saith shall come to pass; he shall have whatsoever he saith.

Some in false humility would argue with Jesus here and beg God to do these things for them instead of commanding them done as He commanded us to do. When we command in obedience, *"thy kingdom come thy will be done on earth as it is in heaven,"* God is the one who does it. In effect; we are commanding Him. Religion will disagree with this but we are supposed to be in relationship with God, co-laborers with Him which therefore causes His kingdom to come.

However, we command what he has told us to command and given us the gift of faith to command. This is what He means by *"concerning the work of My hands command ye me."*

Even though Jesus died in the flesh, He never ceased His ministry. Instead, it became greater for He ministered in His corporate body, as He planned, in order to reach the worldwide, corporate Body of Christ. He continued His ministry in His disciples. He said, *"concerning my sons, and concerning the work of my hands, command ye me."* The Lord's sons do the work of His hands because they are His hands in the earth.

Isaiah 53:10 (KJV)

10 Yet it pleased the Lord to bruise him; he hath put him to grief: when thou shalt make his soul an offering for sin, he shall see his seed, he shall prolong his days, and the pleasure of the Lord shall prosper in his hand.

John 17:21-22 (KJV)

21 That they all may be one; as thou, Father, art in me, and I in thee, that they also may be one in us: that the world may believe that thou hast sent me.

22 And the glory which thou gavest me I have given them; that they may be one, even as we are one:

1 Corinthians 12:12 (KJV)

12 For as the body is one, and hath many members, and all the members of that one body, being many, are one body: so also is Christ.

Matthew 10:40 (KJV)

40 He that receiveth you receiveth me, and he that receiveth me receiveth him that sent me.

His name, Immanuel, means "God with us," and of course He has never left us. Jesus will never leave us nor forsake us. Like as our relationship to Jesus, without the arm, the hand is nothing. The arm gives strength to the hand which was and still is His disciples. *"He shall prolong his days, and the pleasure of the Lord shall prosper in his hand."* As the hands of our Lord, we do all things in accordance with the mind of the Lord and just as He did them when He was physically on earth. Jesus' disciples always commanded healings, deliverances, provisions, and miracles when ministering the gifts of God to others. They prayed for God to do these things in their personal prayer life but not when ministering for they had been given authority to act in Jesus' name.

Acts 3:6 (KJV)

6 Then Peter said, Silver and gold have I none; but such as I have give I thee: In the name of Jesus Christ of Nazareth rise up and walk.

Acts 9:34 (KJV)

34 And Peter said unto him, Aeneas, Jesus Christ maketh thee whole: arise, and make thy bed. And he arose immediately.

Acts 9:40 (KJV)

40 But Peter put them all forth, and kneeled down, and prayed; and turning him to the body said, Tabitha, arise. And she opened her eyes: and when she saw Peter, she sat up.

Understanding Heaven's Court System

Acts 13:11 (KJV)

11 And now, behold, the hand of the Lord is upon thee, and thou shalt be blind, not seeing the sun for a season. And immediately there fell on him a mist and a darkness; and he went about seeking some to lead him by the hand.

Acts 14:9-10 (KJV)

9 The same heard Paul speak: who steadfastly beholding him, and perceiving that he had faith to be healed,

10 Said with a loud voice, Stand upright on thy feet. And he leaped and walked.

Joshua 10:12-13 (KJV)

12 Then spake Joshua to the Lord in the day when the Lord delivered up the Amorites before the children of Israel, and he said in the sight of Israel, Sun, stand thou still upon Gibeon; and thou, Moon, in the valley of Ajalon.

13 And the sun stood still, and the moon stayed, until the people had avenged themselves upon their enemies. Is not this written in the book of Jasher? So the sun stood still in the midst of heaven, and hasted not to go down about a whole day.

Authority is the right to use power and in this case the command to use power. It would have been disobedience to ask God to do what He had commanded them to do. He said, *"Heal the sick, raise the dead, cleanse the lepers, cast out demons: freely ye received, freely give."* and *"As the Father hath sent me, so send I you."*

As Jesus sows the seed of His own life and ministry in His disciples today, it is He that is commanding *"thy kingdom come"* in them, for now, they are the Body of Christ in the earth commanding as He did. Sometimes, this is hard to comprehend but it is what God has intended us to do.

Isaiah 45:3 (KJV)

3 And I will give thee the treasures of darkness, and hidden riches of secret places, that thou mayest know that I, the Lord, which call thee by thy name, am the God of Israel.

God promised that He would give us treasures of darkness and hidden riches of secret places. God has promised us. God is teaching us to pray humbly before Him. We pray specifically for the salvation of our own people and for our salvation. We are exhorted to pray without ceasing. We are urged to become intercessors. So we are praying humbly, pleading with God for our needs and the kingdom's needs.

When it says, "Command ye me", God wants His children to command Him concerning His kingdom's needs and about His own children.

We know that Joshua made use of his right to command God. He had to fight with five kings. The sun was going down before the victory was fully won. He exercised his authority to command the sun not to set. For a whole day, the sun and the moon stood still in their places. To establish God's victory, he commanded the sun to delay its setting. With the extended light, he succeeded in routing the enemy who had come against Israel in full force to hinder the fulfillment of God's promise. But here God says that His children must command Him concerning His promises and concerning His sons and daughters.

Isaiah 65:24 (KJV)

24 And it shall come to pass, that before they call, I will answer; and while they are yet speaking, I will hear.

Whatever we do, we must see victory and fruit. Now, we have got before us a big mountain. We have learned from the Word that if we have faith as a mustard seed, we can remove mountains (Matthew 17:20, 21). Nothing will be impossible when we have that amount of faith.

We have a promise that God has got hidden treasures in secret places for us. We are now constructing this prayer hall for God. It has to be completed in the months ahead.

It will take a great deal of money. Daily, heavy bills will have to be paid. Where is the money? Where is it hid?

God says, "I have got treasures, I will give you treasures of darkness and hidden riches in secret places." Then He says, "Concerning my work, command ye Me." We do not know where this treasure is hid but we know that every type of treasure is hid in Jesus Christ.

It is He that has to supply all our needs. All the materials and the money God has to supply. Our God sustained a nation in the wilderness for forty years by giving angels food, "manna", to them for forty years in the wilderness.

The Lord says, "Command ye Me."

We are not so bold as to command our God. Then what shall we do? Our treasures are with Him. How will it come down to us?

"Just as you rained manna from heaven, rain the money we need." And then God pointed to this verse which says that we must command Him.

So we have the right to claim that our needs be met. We need to be one with God in His work.

Understanding Heaven's Court System

We cannot command God with our limited acquaintance with Him. We must all go to God and get a Word from Him.

We must see that we are right with God. We must grow in understanding and oneness with Him in His work. Without that, we cannot command God.

There is an incident about a man who read of Peter healing a lame man through the power of Jesus. So this man tried to raise a lame man to his feet the same way and he failed miserably. Peter was filled with the Holy Spirit. He was one with Jesus. This gave him the freedom to use the authority and power of Jesus to help that man.

A person who wants to take part in this ministry of prayer must be humble and careful in his walk with God. We should receive promises from God and then lay those promises before God and pray.

God wants us to see His great works. He wants us to be partakers of the great things which He is wanting to show to us. May God bless us all.

Chapter Three

God Will Command His Blessings to Come Upon Us

Blessings don't just come by some kind of chance. They were not just random, chance happenings. They were as deliberate as you can get. God deliberately wanted the blessing to come upon your life. God said that he will command them upon us. How awesome is that? God is in control of the blessing department. Study the context of each of these scriptures.

Leviticus 25:21 (KJV)

21 Then I will command my blessing upon you in the sixth year, and it shall bring forth fruit for three years.

Understanding Heaven's Court System

Deuteronomy 28:8 (KJV)

8 The Lord shall command the blessing upon thee in thy storehouses, and in all that thou settest thine hand unto; and he shall bless thee in the land which the Lord thy God giveth thee.

If this wasn't enough, He also tells us to command him concerning the work of his hands. Command him.

Isaiah 45:11 (KJV)

11 Thus saith the Lord, the Holy One of Israel, and his Maker, Ask me of things to come concerning my sons, and concerning the work of my hands command ye me.

What are the works of his hands that we can command? This is a detail that is much needed.

Deuteronomy 28:12-13 (KJV)

12 The Lord shall open unto thee his good treasure, the heaven to give the rain unto thy land in his season, and to bless all the work of thine hand: and thou shalt lend unto many nations, and thou shalt not borrow.

13 And the Lord shall make thee the head, and not the tail; and thou shalt be above only, and thou shalt not be beneath; if that thou hearken unto the commandments of the Lord thy God, which I command thee this day, to observe and to do them:

All blessings are the result of an action of God who pictures these acts as the work of his hands. God's blessings are the work of His hands. Therefore, the blessings in verses 12-13 above are seen as having come from his hands. So, we can command them according to the word of God in Isaiah 45:11 above.

I will repeat this several different ways because it is time for us all to operate in this level of power in God.

He opens his good treasure unto us. First, he opens his blessing unto us which comes right out of heaven. The two blessings contained there that he commands upon us are the blessing of rain on our land and the blessings upon all the work of our hands. We are authorized to command the good treasure in heaven that gives the rain on our land and the blessings upon all the works of our hands.

He will get us to the place where we do not have to borrow and we can command this. He will bring us into the place where we can lend and we can command this. He will get us to the place where we are the head only and not the tail and the above only

Understanding Heaven's Court System

and not the beneath and we can command both of these. We can command what God said was our promised blessing.

Deuteronomy 28:1-14 (KJV)

1 And it shall come to pass, if thou shalt hearken diligently unto the voice of the Lord thy God, to observe and to do all his commandments which I command thee this day, that the Lord thy God will set thee on high above all nations of the earth:

2 And all these blessings shall come on thee, and overtake thee, if thou shalt hearken unto the voice of the Lord thy God.

3 Blessed shalt thou be in the city, and blessed shalt thou be in the field.

4 Blessed shall be the fruit of thy body, and the fruit of thy ground, and the fruit of thy cattle, the increase of thy kine, and the flocks of thy sheep.

5 Blessed shall be thy basket and thy store.

6 Blessed shalt thou be when thou comest in, and blessed shalt thou be when thou goest out.

7 The Lord shall cause thine enemies that rise up against thee to be smitten before thy face: they shall come out against thee one way, and flee before thee seven ways.

8 The Lord shall command the blessing upon thee in thy storehouses, and in all that thou settest thine hand unto; and he shall bless thee in the land which the Lord thy God giveth thee.

9 The Lord shall establish thee a holy people unto himself, as he hath sworn unto thee, if thou shalt keep the commandments of the Lord thy God, and walk in his ways.

10 And all people of the earth shall see that thou art called by the name of the Lord; and they shall be afraid of thee.

11 And the Lord shall make thee plenteous in goods, in the fruit of thy body, and in the fruit of thy cattle, and in the fruit of thy ground, in the land which the Lord sware unto thy fathers to give thee.

12 The Lord shall open unto thee his good treasure, the heaven to give the rain unto thy land in his season, and to bless all the work of thine hand: and thou shalt lend unto many nations, and thou shalt not borrow.

13 And the Lord shall make thee the head, and not the tail; and thou shalt be above only, and thou shalt not be beneath; if that thou hearken unto the commandments of the Lord thy God, which I command thee this day, to observe and to do them:

14 And thou shalt not go aside from any of the words which I command thee this day, to the right hand, or to the left, to go after other gods to serve them.

We are authorized to command every blessing in there. But there is more.

Understanding Heaven's Court System

Isaiah 45:12-14 (KJV)

12 I have made the earth, and created man upon it: I, even my hands, have stretched out the heavens, and all their host have I commanded.

13 I have raised him up in righteousness, and I will direct all his ways: he shall build my city, and he shall let go my captives, not for price nor reward, saith the Lord of hosts.

14 Thus saith the Lord, The labour of Egypt, and merchandise of Ethiopia and of the Sabeans, men of stature, shall come over unto thee, and they shall be thine: they shall come after thee; in chains they shall come over, and they shall fall down unto thee, they shall make supplication unto thee, saying, Surely God is in thee; and there is none else, there is no God.

We can command everything here because God made it all with his own hands. He commanded it all. Yes. He said we can command it now because it concerns the work of his hands.

Liken and connect the labor of Egypt and the merchandise of Ethiopia and the Sabeans to the verse below.

Bill Vincent

Proverbs 13:22 (KJV)

22 A good man leaveth an inheritance to his children's children: and the wealth of the sinner is laid up for the just.

The wealth of the sinner, including the Egyptians and the Sabeans, is laid up to the just. The wealth of the wicked is laid up for the righteous. We can command this too.

Now see this: sometimes God starts us out in a smaller place than we want to be. We humans always want to be higher up the level than we sometimes are, don't we? Nevertheless, don't look at your small place as permanent. God has no joy in seeing you down. He made you to be above and not beneath. Your small place is temporary. You can command this too. This is worth reading again.

Suppose you just started the business you have wanted for so long. Then recession hits and just destroys everything. You are forced to find and secure a job. It doesn't pay much. You are in a small place. Remember this. God created that job with his own hands. Command it. Tell it what to do. Then when God says in your heart that the time is right, you will start your business again. God created your job with his hands. Command it. Think about it.

Understanding Heaven's Court System

Chapter Four

Court System of Heaven

It is time to go to court. The Court System of heaven is higher than the Supreme Court in the United States of America is. God is calling us to engage Mount Zion; to literally go into the Heavenly Zion and to learn how to engage with and become part of the Courts of Heaven and His Government. Mountains speak of governmental realms and this is His governmental arena where we come to release legislation into the earth and to annul the contracts of Satan made against us.

This was a lot to contain the first time I heard this but here is your invitation to come up higher and become a part of the court system of heaven.

Zechariah 3:7 (KJV)

7 Thus saith the Lord of hosts; If thou wilt walk in my ways, and if thou wilt keep my charge, then thou shalt also judge my house, and shalt also keep my

Understanding Heaven's Court System

courts, and I will give thee places to walk among these that stand by.

Isaiah 2:3 (KJV)

3 And many people shall go and say, Come ye, and let us go up to the mountain of the Lord, to the house of the God of Jacob; and he will teach us of his ways, and we will walk in his paths: for out of Zion shall go forth the law, and the word of the Lord from Jerusalem.

Hebrews 12:22-24(KJV)

22 But ye are come unto mount Sion, and unto the city of the living God, the heavenly Jerusalem, and to an innumerable company of angels,

23 To the general assembly and church of the firstborn, which are written in heaven, and to God the Judge of all, and to the spirits of just men made perfect,

24 And to Jesus the mediator of the new covenant, and to the blood of sprinkling, that speaketh better things than that of Abel.

I will build my church (ecclesia = legislative, judicial government) and the gates of hell shall not prevail against it.

Matthew 16:18 (KJV)

18 And I say also unto thee, That thou art Peter, and upon this rock I will build my church; and the gates of hell shall not prevail against it.

Jeremiah 23:18 (KJV)

18 For who hath stood in the counsel of the Lord, and hath perceived and heard his word? Who hath marked his word, and heard it?

God is raising up His Government on the earth and teaching us how to engage the courtroom of heaven and have things change in a massive way personally and nationally. The revelation of the court system of heaven really can change everything in your life and the nations. A foundation; the idea of courtroom and justice is all through the Bible.

Psalm 89:14 (KJV)

14 Justice and judgment are the habitation of thy throne: mercy and truth shall go before thy face.

God is very much interested in the right thing happening and justice for his creation. Just and Righteous is who He is not just what He does! He

Himself has a throne where He rules and that rule is based on Righteousness and Justice. Everyone has had things stolen from them and experienced unjust situations and/or circumstances! This can fall in the categories of health, destinies, inheritances or dreams. Revivals in the past have been attacked and ultimately ended prematurely. Nations that were supposed to prosper have struggled with poverty instead.

I just heard one of the most powerful sermons by Nathan Morris of Shake The Nations Ministries. He spoke of reclaiming our territories. This is perfect for heaven's court. Reclaiming territories lost for your family, ministry or personally. It is time to reclaim our territories.

The church itself is not walking in the power of the early apostolic era. Anything that is living short of what God wants us to live like is an injustice and therefore not right in God's eyes. The truth is we have been stolen from in a lot of areas but this is the time where the books in heaven are being opened and God is about to render a verdict on our behalf!

Apostle John and Daniel both saw such a time where the saints of God would be given justice in the courts of heaven! If God did it then, He'll do it today. The amazing thing is the courtroom is rigged on our behalf because the Judge is actually our father our advocate is Jesus and the word of God is our Bill of Rights.

Zechariah 3:1-7 (KJV)

3 And he shewed me Joshua the high priest standing before the angel of the Lord, and Satan standing at his right hand to resist him.

2 And the Lord said unto Satan, The Lord rebuke thee, O Satan; even the Lord that hath chosen Jerusalem rebuke thee: is not this a brand plucked out of the fire?

3 Now Joshua was clothed with filthy garments, and stood before the angel.

4 And he answered and spake unto those that stood before him, saying, Take away the filthy garments from him. And unto him he said, Behold, I have caused thine iniquity to pass from thee, and I will clothe thee with change of raiment.

5 And I said, Let them set a fair mitre upon his head. So they set a fair mitre upon his head, and clothed him with garments. And the angel of the Lord stood by.

6 And the angel of the Lord protested unto Joshua, saying,

7 Thus saith the Lord of hosts; If thou wilt walk in my ways, and if thou wilt keep my charge, then thou shalt also judge my house, and shalt also keep my courts, and I will give thee places to walk among these that stand by.

Some keys to remember: God is the Ultimate Judge and Jesus intercedes on your behalf like a lawyer in court defends you. The accuser is the devil that accuses the saints.

As we just saw in scriptures above, they put a clean new turban on his head. Then they finished dressing him with God's angel looking on.

Joshua was promised access to Heaven and access to the courtroom if he was obedient to God's ways. And this promise is for us too because all the promises in God are yes and amen! We can all go into the courtroom no matter how dirty or unclean we feel and what filthy rags we think we are wearing. You don't get clean to go to the court; you go to the court and you will get clean. The Word of God explains that the blood of Jesus is in the courtroom of Heaven. Joshua wasn't clean when he went to the court but he was given new robes representing forgiveness and the washing of the blood that makes us white as snow! And just like Joshua, we will be given a new turban which represents the mind of Christ. And it gets even better! The promise wasn't just that we can go to court to petition but that if we live the way He tells us then we can oversee the affairs of the Judge and make the decisions! That is a realm of government that very few have walked in that's for sure but yet the promise is there for all to see! So it's not just about us going in and pleading, it starts off there of course, but we're going to rule and reign and be part of the justice system. We are kings and priests of our God and we are going to participate in the government of heaven invading the earth. What amazing days we live in!

Let's look at another Court of Heaven experience.

Job 1:6-8 (KJV)

6 Now there was a day when the sons of God came to present themselves before the Lord, and Satan came also among them.

7 And the Lord said unto Satan, Whence comest thou? Then Satan answered the Lord, and said, From going to and fro in the earth, and from walking up and down in it.

8 And the Lord said unto Satan, Hast thou considered my servant Job, that there is none like him in the earth, a perfect and an upright man, one that feareth God, and escheweth evil?

Job 2:1-8 (KJV)

Again there was a day when the sons of God came to present themselves before the Lord, and Satan came also among them to present himself before the Lord.

2 And the Lord said unto Satan, From whence comest thou? And Satan answered the Lord, and said, From going to and fro in the earth, and from walking up and down in it.

3 And the Lord said unto Satan, Hast thou considered my servant Job, that there is none like

Understanding Heaven's Court System

him in the earth, a perfect and an upright man, one that feareth God, and escheweth evil? and still he holdeth fast his integrity, although thou movedst me against him, to destroy him without cause.

4 And Satan answered the Lord, and said, Skin for skin, yea, all that a man hath will he give for his life.

5 But put forth thine hand now, and touch his bone and his flesh, and he will curse thee to thy face.

6 And the Lord said unto Satan, Behold, he is in thine hand; but save his life.

7 So went Satan forth from the presence of the Lord, and smote Job with sore boils from the sole of his foot unto his crown.

8 And he took him a potsherd to scrape himself withal; and he sat down among the ashes.

Satan is the designated accuser and that he comes to the heavenly court. An accuser is courtroom language! An accuser is someone who has a case against you or at least has some accusations to present against an individual, family or even a nation. This is where the devil has the right to accuse us. We also see that the court is where Satan got permission to curse Job and strike him with severe sores. For it was God who said "alright. Go ahead- you can do what you like with him but mind you, don't kill him."

Whether we realize it or not, Satan has been going to the courtroom, just like he did with Job, to get permission to steal from all of our lives. And because no one has been going into court and saying no we want to present our case and oppose what the accuser is saying, we have experienced defeat after defeat! We have often perished because of lack of knowledge. However, the good news is this is changing rapidly!! There is now a growing company of people on this earth who are engaging in the heavenly courts and learning how to participate and function there to bring justice to the earth!! His Government will rule from shore to shore and of the increase of His government, there will be no end! The Government might be on His shoulders but we are His body! We are learning how to rule and reign!! So here is a New Testament example of the courtroom.

Luke 22:31-34 (KJV)

31 And the Lord said, Simon, Simon, behold, Satan hath desired to have you, that he may sift you as wheat:

32 But I have prayed for thee, that thy faith fail not: and when thou art converted, strengthen thy brethren.

33 And he said unto him, Lord, I am ready to go with thee, both into prison, and to death.

Understanding Heaven's Court System

34 And he said, I tell thee, Peter, the cock shall not crow this day, before that thou shalt thrice deny that thou knowest me.

In this example, Satan asked to sift them all like grain. Satan asked excessively. In simple terms, this means that Satan asked many times if he could destroy the disciples. What I want to ask then is this, where did he ask? Well, the answer is also simple. In the courts, of course! All through the Bible examples, the courts are always where Satan asks for permission to do things on earth! And it's obvious that it is in the courts that Satan asks to destroy us too.

Revelation 12:10 (KJV)

10 And I heard a loud voice saying in heaven, Now is come salvation, and strength, and the kingdom of our God, and the power of his Christ: for the accuser of our brethren is cast down, which accused them before our God day and night.

Satan doesn't just make accusations against us but he makes them against us day and night. This happens while the church sleeps. We can also see that he brings charges against us! Again, that is courtroom language! There is a day coming when the courtroom will be in place and the accuser of the brethren will be cast down. But until that day, we need to learn how to engage the courtrooms of heaven to enable the judge to make a verdict on our behalf! The Judge is Father God.

The Lord is our advocate. An advocate is someone who speaks on behalf of someone else. The term is often used in the legal profession to describe someone who has received some legal training which allows him or her to represent another in a courtroom. So basically scripture is saying that Jesus is legally trained and he knows how to represent you in the court. So, if you fall short and sin, Jesus can represent you in the court and your forgiveness is guaranteed because He took the punishment you deserved!

The whole court system is rigged on our behalf. The idea of the courtroom is all through scripture. Imagine going to court in America and knowing you will win. If your case is backed by the Word of God, then you have a rigged court of heaven to present your case.

Amos 5:15

Hate evil, love good; maintain justice in the courts

Understanding Heaven's Court System

Psalm 100:4 (KJV)

4 Enter into his gates with thanksgiving, and into his courts with praise: be thankful unto him, and bless his name.

Psalm 35:1 (KJV)

Plead my cause, O Lord, with them that strive with me: fight against them that fight against me.

Job 13:18 (KJV)

18 Behold now, I have ordered my cause; I know that I shall be justified.

In the two scriptures about Job, Satan appeared in the courtroom and asked to harm Job. And he did harm Job but do you think from this scripture that Job has learned a valuable piece of wisdom? He says now that I have prepared my case I know that I will be vindicated! This is court system terms. What would have happened if Job had prepared his case earlier? Would he have been vindicated earlier before all the boils and death? Would he have been able to block Satan's attempt to destroy him and his family in the court? Who knows for sure but Job was certain that now his case was made, he would be vindicated! It's time for us to learn that lesson and make our cases in court!

There are some things I want to highlight about the scriptures.

- There is a courtroom in heaven that we all have full access too.

- Satan goes to the courtroom to accuse us day and night. This happens whether we have this revelation or not.

- Satan looks for any legal gap so that he can ask permission to attack your life. He wants to steal kill and destroy and because we haven't known about the courtroom, he has often been successful.

- We have been invited to take part in the courtroom. The invitation is available to all of God's children.

- We don't need to be clean to go to the courtroom. We are made clean when we go there! Joshua was given new garments. The blood of Jesus is available to cleanse us when we go to court.

- We defeat principalities and powers and the devil in the courtroom. This is the ultimate warfare. That's where true authority is!

It's like a policeman standing in the road with his hand up, he doesn't have much power in himself but he does have the whole backing of the law behind him! Therefore, because the whole law is behind him, you probably will stop when he simply lifts his hand. That's what authority is. When we get the scrolls and papers from heaven that declare your unjust situation must change, you better believe they have to change because no demon in hell dares stand against that decree and verdict of the court! All of heaven backs that verdict including angels and the Ancient of Days Himself! I just want to say, "Wooooo!"

- We can ask for 7 times back what has been stolen from us! And, all the substance of his house. This is our God-given biblical right.

Proverbs 6:31 (KJV)

31 But if he be found, he shall restore sevenfold; he shall give all the substance of his house.

That's not only what he's stolen from you, but that's also the booty, spoils of war, and the plunder! Imagine if we got back everything that the enemy has stolen times 7? I like to imagine, wonder and ask questions when I study the Word of God. Imagine all those revivals that were cut short? Imagine what the apostolic fathers walked in? Imagine what Maria Woodworth Etter walked in and William Branham? Or even Smith

Wigglesworth. Imagine if we not only get back what they walked in but 7 times more?

Daniel 7:9-11 (KJV)

9 I beheld till the thrones were cast down, and the Ancient of Days did sit, whose garment was white as snow, and the hair of his head like the pure wool: his throne was like the fiery flame, and his wheels as burning fire.

10 A fiery stream issued and came forth from before him: thousand thousands ministered unto him, and ten thousand times ten thousand stood before him: the judgment was set, and the books were opened.

11 I beheld then because of the voice of the great words which the horn spake: I beheld even till the beast was slain, and his body destroyed, and given to the burning flame.

Daniel says he saw thrones that were placed, not just a singular throne for the Lord, but plural, thrones. Who are the thrones for? The answer is you and me! Yes, you did read that right. He is the **K**ing of **K**ings but we are **k**ings. I like to call us little **k**ings of the one and only God. He's the **L**ord of **L**ords but we are **l**ords! We are seated at the right hand of God. Seated is symbolic of authority! The thrones are there for us! We are supposed to be seated in heavenly places. We need to walk in this, hunger for this, desire this and honor this.

Understanding Heaven's Court System

We need to ask the Lord to teach us how to engage the courtroom, seven spirits of God to come and teach us. You may say but I don't understand anything about this but that's what the 7 spirits are coming to train and teach us! There are books or what I like to refer to as scrolls being opened in heaven right now. This is the time Daniel was talking about. God doesn't take away authority until there are people who can take that place of authority. God couldn't put David in place until he was ready to rule as a King. He was called to be King but had to be prepared to rule as King. He couldn't replace Saul until David was ready. And this is the right time.

There is a company of people who are getting ready to rule and reign with Christ! There is a generation who will take back all that's been stolen! For generations, we the saints have been stolen from and we have suffered injustice in many ways. The courts of heaven bring justice. But in these last days, the Ancient of Days is about to open the books (scrolls) and He is going to release justice and we will reap what many generations have sown. One generation will receive all the rewards of all the prayers made by all the saints down throughout the ages. Every promise ever made to any saint will be fulfilled! And we, the end time bride will be the beneficiaries! It's justice time! And we are about to receive a verdict in our favor! We have a lot of justice way overdue.

So practically how do we access the courtroom? Simply by faith. It doesn't matter what you feel or don't feel. The Bible says that by faith, Enoch was translated! We need to just believe that it's real because it is and our physical senses will catch up sometime! So, when you go into court, you have an attitude of honor. It's not a formula remember but there are some simple protocols! When we see America's courts there is honor and respect. The same goes for heaven. So I honor the judge, the court, sometimes the angels and the cloud of witnesses. When I enter the courts, I might say, "I thank you, Father God, for hearing my petition before the court of heaven." It is about honor. Let the Holy Spirit teach you because we are all different and it is not a formula. I enter with thanksgiving. It is okay to say thanks to the court for hearing our cry.

Remember, we must judge ourselves first, admit the sin, ask God to cleanse you; the blood is there for you and it speaks on your behalf. Then, I would simply present my case to the Judge. For example, let's say the injustice is sickness. I would find all the scriptures about sickness and build up a case; by His stripes, we are healed, he bore all our sicknesses and took our infirmities. I would simply present them to the judge and ask Him to judge the sickness. I would say something like your word says it is unjust that I should be sick, that by your stripes I am supposed to be healed. You're building up a case and simply

Understanding Heaven's Court System

presenting it to the judge. This can work for anything, whether its poverty, financial difficulties, or a region that needs a breakthrough in some way. This is not a formula, the Lord may lead you in a different way and that's all ok as long as we remain humble and teachable, we won't go wrong.

Intimacy is key! This is what makes this so powerful. God requires intimacy and a humble heart. When we go to court, we humble ourselves and cleanse ourselves. It is all about intimacy.

He will lead you and teach you! Build a history in the courts. Go often. The more cases you present, the more you win and the more you will be known in heaven's court system. How do we know what we have the right to ask for in the courtroom? The promises in God are yes and amen. You can ask for every promise in the Bible; it's all yours!

2 Corinthians 1:20 (KJV)

20 For all the promises of God in him are yea, and in him Amen, unto the glory of God by us.

Your scroll and blueprints are what God spoke to you about concerning your life. So let me ask questions. What has God spoken over your life? What dreams have you had about your life? What prophecies have you received? What promises has

God made to you? Don't worry about making mistakes. "The future belongs to the courageous!" God's government is coming and He is calling the weak, the broken. He's calling the uneducated. His voice is calling from heaven. Can you hear it? Not many wise are called to this! God chooses the foolish to confound the wise. But if we choose to be foolish enough to believe that we can participate in heaven's government and heaven's courts then we will be chosen to participate in the greatest age mankind has ever seen! The age of the ecclesia, the age of the manifestation of the sons of God ruling reigning and governing in union with Him! This is the courtroom of heaven. The Court of Heaven is a place to take care of business or legal matters in the heavenly place and see things change on the earth that otherwise may never have changed. If it gets settled in heaven, things change on the earth pretty fast and miraculously. Jesus' blood gives us access.

There is no waiting time to get into the courtroom; the doors are always open. God is the Judge.

James 4:12 (KJV)

12 There is one lawgiver, who is able to save and to destroy: who art thou that judgeth another?

Jesus is our Advocate.

Understanding Heaven's Court System

1 John 2:1 (KJV)

2 My little children, these things write I unto you, that ye sin not. And if any man sin, we have an advocate with the Father, Jesus Christ the righteous:

Satan, which is the accuser of the brethren, is the opposing attorney. He is making accusations against us stating that you deserve punishment.

We present our case before the Judge, countering with the argument that the Blood of Jesus and repentance brings "legal" forgiveness or justification.

Romans 5:9 (KJV)

9 Much more then, being now justified by his blood, we shall be saved from wrath through him.

The Judge makes his final verdict. The courts of heaven are heavily stacked in our favor as long as we follow the proper protocols. We can't really lose as long as we show up.

Job presented arguments for his case, pleading to go straight to the Judge of heaven and earth to plead his case.

Job 13:3 (KJV)

Surely I would speak to the Almighty, and I desire to reason with God.

Job knew that true justice would only come from the true Judge of heaven and earth. It goes so far as to say that the Judge will even deliver those that are not innocent.

Job 22:30 (KJV)

30 He shall deliver the island of the innocent: and it is delivered by the pureness of thine hands.

Is one time in the courts enough? The persistent widow kept pleading her case with the Judge until he gave in. How much more will the Judge of heaven and earth answer us?

Luke 18:1-8 (KJV)

And he spake a parable unto them to this end, that men ought always to pray, and not to faint;

2 Saying, There was in a city a judge, which feared not God, neither regarded man:

3 And there was a widow in that city; and she came unto him, saying, Avenge me of mine adversary.

Understanding Heaven's Court System

4 And he would not for a while: but afterward he said within himself, Though I fear not God, nor regard man;

5 Yet because this widow troubleth me, I will avenge her, lest by her continual coming she weary me.

6 And the Lord said, Hear what the unjust judge saith.

7 And shall not God avenge his own elect, which cry day and night unto him, though he bear long with them?

8 I tell you that he will avenge them speedily. Nevertheless when the Son of man cometh, shall he find faith on the earth?

Job was very persistent, *"I'm not letting up. I'm standing my ground. My complaint is legitimate." (Job 23:1)*

"If only I knew where to find God, I would go to his court. I would lay out my case and present my arguments." (Job 23:3-4)

The accuser of the brethren is always there to accuse us before the Judge. All we have to do is show up covered in the blood, having already repented, and presenting our case. If the enemy tries to bring up our past or any past sins in our life that have already been repented of and forgiven, the Judge won't allow them to be used against us as evidence. They are already covered under the blood, paid for, repented and forgiven. Most Christians lose battles on the earth simply by not showing up to the courts of heaven. The devil is a legalist and tries to find a loophole. The only loophole he can use is if you don't show up and plead your case or if you don't repent of anything he could use against you.

Matthew 5:25 (KJV)

25 Agree with thine adversary quickly, whiles thou art in the way with him; lest at any time the adversary deliver thee to the judge, and the judge deliver thee to the officer, and thou be cast into prison.

Just as with Job, the enemy has to get permission from God even to afflict you. Jesus told Peter that Satan has asked for permission to sift you like wheat.

Luke 22:31 (KJV)

31 And the Lord said, Simon, Simon, behold, Satan hath desired to have you, that he may sift you as wheat:

Understanding Heaven's Court System

The accuser of the brethren accuses God's people day and night.

Revelation 12:10 (KJV)

10 And I heard a loud voice saying in heaven, Now is come salvation, and strength, and the kingdom of our God, and the power of his Christ: for the accuser of our brethren is cast down, which accused them before our God day and night.

One important key is to prepare your case with as much evidence as possible. Gather scriptures, prophetic words, witnesses-angels, the cloud of witnesses, etc.

Job said, "Now that I have prepared my case, I know I'll be vindicated." Once you win your case in the heavenly courtroom and have defeated even principalities and powers, you are given a heavenly scroll with the final verdict. Now you have true authority. Show these papers and legal documents to the powers of darkness. They know they have no more legal authority to attack you. All heaven is now ordered to back you up. Demand your enemy to restore sevenfold and all the substance of his house. Booty which is spoils of war and plunder.

You don't have to finish this book to get started. I used to read a lot of books and highlight and write in the book to make it my handbook to help me grow. I encourage you to do this.

Understanding Heaven's Court System

Chapter Five

Prophetic Decrees

We all can release prophetic decrees. This is vital in getting things done fast. How many prophetic promises and words were spoken over your life, have you yet to see come to pass? Every believer has prophetic promises from heaven whether God has revealed something that we would accomplish for Him, something that we would become, or something that we would see Him do in our lifetime.

Prophetic words are authoritative words that scripture says we would "do well to pay attention to."

2 Peter 1:19 (KJV)

19 We have also a more sure word of prophecy; whereunto ye do well that ye take heed, as unto a light that shineth in a dark place, until the day dawn, and the day star arise in your hearts:

Understanding Heaven's Court System

Many believers have waited years to realize the fulfillment of prophetic words spoken over them or revelations from visions or dreams. Do you ever wonder what to do with them, how to act upon them, or how to ensure the fulfillment of them in your life or ministry? How do we bring the words of the Lord to pass? What hinders the fulfillment of them?

Some blame the delay on the prophet or the person who delivered the word and others blame themselves. Sadly, many give up believing their promises. However, delay in the fulfillment of a heavenly word spoken over you may have everything to do with the enemy; opposing, dark, spiritual forces determined to sabotage your destiny. Then the delay does have something to do with us for the delay is in our lack of response. We give up waiting or we don't determine that "word" really was for us and give up on the vision.

We don't do what God has called us to do because our mindsets aren't in line with the potential God gives us. We're not responding by pulling from heaven "those things that be not as though they were."

There are things that have always been in the eternal purpose of God, it's just that they're not in our natural realm yet. But the promises of God have always been in God's heart, even before the foundation of the world. Everything we need in the natural to do what God has called us to do is available in the invisible realm. We must learn how to see the promises of God in the invisible by the eye of faith, embrace it in the invisible, and bring it to the earth. Embrace, confess, and declare God's promises into the heavens!

This is a powerful tool if you can take hold of it. Prophetic decrees made into the heavens have the power to transform your life! Heavenly prophetic decrees and proclamations hasten the fulfillment of God's word over your life. They're powerful! They ruin the plans of the enemy and accelerate the birth and fulfillment of every prophetic promise and revelation spoken over you!

When I learned how to make prophetic decrees and proclamations in my own life, God was able to do a whole lot faster in me and through me.

Through our prophetic decrees, God also releases angels to battle the forces of the enemy to bring us what is rightfully ours! That's part of their job description! I hope to give some insight into this on how you can make prophetic decrees and proclamations into the heavens, which will hasten and bring to pass the word of the Lord. I want you to understand your responsibility with God-given promises and visions and how you can partner with God to realize your destiny.

The Bible speaks of our responsibility with the Word of the Lord. When Jesus came into the region of Caesarea Philippi, He asked His disciples, saying, *"Who do men say that I, the Son of Man, am?"* So they said, *"Some say John the Baptist, some Elijah, and others Jeremiah or one of the prophets."* He said to them, *"But who do you say that I am?"* Simon Peter answered and said, *"You are the Christ, the Son of the living God."*

Matthew 16:13-19 (KJV)

13 When Jesus came into the coasts of Caesarea Philippi, he asked his disciples, saying, Whom do men say that I the Son of man am?

14 And they said, Some say that thou art John the Baptist: some, Elias; and others, Jeremias, or one of the prophets.

15 He saith unto them, But whom say ye that I am?

16 And Simon Peter answered and said, Thou art the Christ, the Son of the living God.

17 And Jesus answered and said unto him, Blessed art thou, Simon Barjona: for flesh and blood hath not revealed it unto thee, but my Father which is in heaven.

18 And I say also unto thee, That thou art Peter, and upon this rock I will build my church; and the gates of hell shall not prevail against it.

19 And I will give unto thee the keys of the kingdom of heaven: and whatsoever thou shalt bind on earth shall be bound in heaven: and whatsoever thou shalt loose on earth shall be loosed in heaven.

Take note of one thought in this passage: *"Peter, flesh, and blood have not revealed this to you, but my Father who is in heaven."* Peter's revelation came from heaven. You may also have received divine inspiration like Peter, a prophetic word, a vision or, perhaps, an illumined scripture from God.

Maybe a prophet called you out and prophesied over you or God spoke to you through television or a dream. Prophetic words and promises are personal, specific to our lives as individuals, our families, or our ministries. They may also be intended for cities, regions, peoples, and nations. They are always in line with the Word, the Bible from Genesis through to Revelation. However, I want to focus primarily on those words that God has given to us personally, those Rhema words. Rhema words and God's Word are a powerful combination that can activate our divine destiny.

Let's look at this again.

Matthew 16:18 (KJV)

*18 And I say also unto thee, That thou art Peter, and **upon this rock** I will build my church; and the gates of hell shall not prevail against it.*

Now, what does Jesus mean by the words "on this rock"? I know a prophet that believes that this is referring to the Office of the Apostle. This is

Understanding Heaven's Court System

because Peter became an apostle. However, I don't believe Peter or the apostles are the rock. I believe Jesus is saying, "Upon this rock, the rock of revelation I am building... Upon the rock of being able to hear what your Father in heaven is saying. Flesh and blood has not revealed this unto you. Upon that rock, I shall build My church."

In the book of Jeremiah, the Bible also tells us that the purpose of the Lord is to build you and not pull you down, plant you and not pluck you up.

Jeremiah 24:6 (KJV)

6 For I will set mine eyes upon them for good, and I will bring them again to this land: and I will build them, and not pull them down; and I will plant them, and not pluck them up.

Jeremiah 42:10 (KJV)

10 If ye will still abide in this land, then will I build you, and not pull you down, and I will plant you, and not pluck you up: for I repent me of the evil that I have done unto you.

So, when God gives you a heavenly revelation, it's to build you and plant you. It's to build and plant something in you and through you. It's to build, plant, loose, birth, and bring to pass His Word with the help of the Holy Ghost. Equally, there are some things we have to tear down in the spirit, those forces opposing the fulfillment of God's Word.

Later, in Matthew 16 Jesus says, "Peter, I've given you the keys, the keys to the kingdom."

Matthew 16:19 (KJV)

19 And I will give unto thee the keys of the kingdom of heaven: and whatsoever thou shalt bind on earth shall be bound in heaven: and whatsoever thou shalt loose on earth shall be loosed in heaven.

Do you know what the keys are?

They are every prophetic word that you have, yes, every revelation you have ever received. Some of us in the Body of Christ run around with a keychain full of keys like a janitor with keys wherever we go. Maybe you have a whole lot of keys on your key chain. Perhaps, you don't even know which one fits which lock! Sure, you used to know but many of those keys have been there a long time, so long that you don't even know what they're for anymore. Why have fifty keys on your keychain if you only use a few?

Every time we receive a prophetic word, we add a key to our ring. It's a key to the kingdom, your kingdom. It's key to destiny. I'm not talking about those that prophesy to you and are not Words from God. When the Words are pure and powerful straight from God then it's a key for you to open up the heavens and loose things in heaven so what God said about you in heaven can come to pass on the earth. With that destiny word, you can build or pull-down, plant or pluck up and bring destiny to its fulfillment. That is what we're supposed to be using the keys for. How many keys are you carrying? You need to discover what they go to.

Properly learn how to use the keys handed to you through visions, dreams, or words from the Lord. That's what Jesus taught Peter. The Lord's message was: "Peter these are keys. I just gave you a key called "revelation." With that key, you have a responsibility to open up the Kingdom of Heaven so that revelation can come to pass."

Rest assured that God usually only shows you something He wants you to have now, not fifty years from now. Yes, He has a timetable but I don't believe His intention is to dangle a carrot on a string in front of your nose! I don't believe He works that way. Delays often happen not because of the prophet or because of "God's timing," or the devil, but because of us. When God speaks to us, He's not asking us to believe that we can. He's trying to change our identity so that we will. When He gives us a prophetic word, it becomes potential. It becomes a desire that He plants in us. It's key to bring our destiny to pass.

We have a responsibility to birth God's prophetic Word and promises. When God speaks something for us, He is releasing potential in us; He's giving us a key to unlock that possibility. But we must posture ourselves to realize that potential.

The fulfillment of prophetic words is conditional, in as much as we are required to respond and take certain steps of obedience. I believe that once we get to heaven, we'll discover how much more God had for us in this life that we never realized or saw to completion. Many Christians wonder why their dreams are not yet fulfilled. They have good intentions but never walk out what God has for them. God's reason for giving us these revelatory keys is to excite, edify, and encourage us to press on toward the mark; they are filled with possibility.

Study Daniel. He had a revelation while he was reading the book of Jeremiah.

Daniel 9:2 (KJV)

2 In the first year of his reign I Daniel understood by books the number of the years, whereof the word of the Lord came to Jeremiah the prophet, that he would accomplish seventy years in the desolations of Jerusalem.

Understanding Heaven's Court System

As he read, God came along, breathed on the scripture and said, "Daniel, what Jeremiah prophesied about the Babylonian captivity, that's your generation. You are about to come out of Babylonian captivity after 70 years."

Daniel didn't just proclaim the news; he birthed it through fasting and prayer.

Daniel 10 (KJV)

In the third year of Cyrus king of Persia a thing was revealed unto Daniel, whose name was called Belteshazzar; and the thing was true, but the time appointed was long: and he understood the thing, and had understanding of the vision.

2 In those days I Daniel was mourning three full weeks.

3 I ate no pleasant bread, neither came flesh nor wine in my mouth, neither did I anoint myself at all, till three whole weeks were fulfilled.

4 And in the four and twentieth day of the first month, as I was by the side of the great river, which is Hiddekel;

5 Then I lifted up mine eyes, and looked, and behold a certain man clothed in linen, whose loins were girded with fine gold of Uphaz:

6 His body also was like the beryl, and his face as the appearance of lightning, and his eyes as lamps of fire, and his arms and his feet like in colour to polished brass, and the voice of his words like the voice of a multitude.

7 And I Daniel alone saw the vision: for the men that were with me saw not the vision; but a great quaking fell upon them, so that they fled to hide themselves.

8 Therefore I was left alone, and saw this great vision, and there remained no strength in me: for my comeliness was turned in me into corruption, and I retained no strength.

9 Yet heard I the voice of his words: and when I heard the voice of his words, then was I in a deep sleep on my face, and my face toward the ground.

10 And, behold, a hand touched me, which set me upon my knees and upon the palms of my hands.

11 And he said unto me, O Daniel, a man greatly beloved, understand the words that I speak unto thee, and stand upright: for unto thee am I now sent. And when he had spoken this word unto me, I stood trembling.

12 Then said he unto me, Fear not, Daniel: for from the first day that thou didst set thine heart to understand, and to chasten thyself before thy God, thy words were heard, and I am come for thy words.

13 But the prince of the kingdom of Persia withstood me one and twenty days: but, lo, Michael, one of the chief princes, came to help me; and I remained there with the kings of Persia.

Understanding Heaven's Court System

14 Now I am come to make thee understand what shall befall thy people in the latter days: for yet the vision is for many days.

15 And when he had spoken such words unto me, I set my face toward the ground, and I became dumb.

16 And, behold, one like the similitude of the sons of men touched my lips: then I opened my mouth, and spake, and said unto him that stood before me, O my lord, by the vision my sorrows are turned upon me, and I have retained no strength.

17 For how can the servant of this my lord talk with this my lord? for as for me, straightway there remained no strength in me, neither is there breath left in me.

18 Then there came again and touched me one like the appearance of a man, and he strengthened me,

19 And said, O man greatly beloved, fear not: peace be unto thee, be strong, yea, be strong. And when he had spoken unto me, I was strengthened, and said, Let my lord speak; for thou hast strengthened me.

20 Then said he, Knowest thou wherefore I come unto thee? and now will I return to fight with the prince of Persia: and when I am gone forth, lo, the prince of Grecia shall come.

21 But I will shew thee that which is noted in the scripture of truth: and there is none that holdeth with me in these things, but Michael your prince.

He grabbed hold of it, responded, and became involved in God's Word. God said it and so now, he needed to lay hold of what He said. Like Daniel, we must also birth these prophetic words of God. It's not a matter of, "Well, God said it so He's going to do it. His sovereignty will bring it to pass. I'm just going to wait and see."

The prophet delivers God's potential for us, why stone the prophet if things don't happen? The purpose of the prophetic is to stir and cause destiny to come alive in you so you'll become passionate about the potential God planted in you.

Daniel hears God's promise of release from Babylonian captivity and he says, "Okay. Now I need to do my part. It's not just good enough that God spoke. I need to pray and fast it through."

What if Daniel said, "Well, perhaps God didn't really mean anything by this. I'm not sure it's going to happen. It's not happening! If it was God, it should have happened already! I mean, God said it!" No, Daniel didn't give up, he kept praying and after twenty-one days, Michael the archangel appeared and said *paraphrased*, "Daniel, come over here for a minute. Let me tell you something. God heard you on the first day. But you see, we ran into some opposition in heaven called the Prince of Persia. The enemy didn't want you to receive what God wanted you to have twenty-one days ago so there was a delay in the spirit."

Understanding Heaven's Court System

It's not that the Word wasn't of God. It's not that the prophet was wrong. But there was a delay in the spirit. Think about your prophetic promises. There might be some devils today holding back what is rightfully yours. There is a Prince of Persia in the spiritual realm. I want you to know that God heard you the first day. You should have seen the fulfillment years ago but it hasn't come yet. It's not God. It's not you. It's the devil resisting your destiny, tying it up in the spirit. If it happened to Daniel, it can happen to us. God had to send Michael to battle through that Prince of the enemy. Let me tell you something if the devil came against Jesus and against Moses, he is warring against all of God's people. The devil wants to kill every move of God in its infancy. He wants to discourage you right when you get saved or right when you get healed. He wants to try taking God's blessings from you.

Back when God's people were captive in Egypt, Satan knew something was going on. He knew the prophetic words of Joseph and that they would return to the land of which God swore to Abraham, to Isaac, and to Jacob.

Genesis 50:24 (KJV)

24 And Joseph said unto his brethren, I die: and God will surely visit you, and bring you out of this land unto the land which he sware to Abraham, to Isaac, and to Jacob.

So when Moses was born Satan said, "We need to issue a decree. We need to kill all the male children under two-years-old. We are going to kill him." That's when God had to orchestrate the deliverance of the baby Moses. After that attempt on Moses' life, the devil tried the same tactic on Jesus.

Matthew 2:16 (KJV)

16 Then Herod, when he saw that he was mocked of the wise men, was exceeding wroth, and sent forth, and slew all the children that were in Bethlehem, and in all the coasts thereof, from two years old and under, according to the time which he had diligently inquired of the wise men.

Revelation 12:17 (KJV)

17 And the dragon was wroth with the woman, and went to make war with the remnant of her seed, which keep the commandments of God, and have the testimony of Jesus Christ.

Satan knows that God has a plan for us. Satan has a plan of destruction. He is not just going to lie down, roll over, and let you be what God wants you to be. He is working overtime to distract you and to delay the fulfillment of your promises. He is working overtime to sideline you or to kill, steal and destroy in your life. Satan has assigned demonic cohorts in the spiritual realm to keep you from finding the revelation of God's will. And when you do find it, he stirs up a whole lot of mess to get you so distracted that you can't really press on "toward the goal for the prize of the call of God in Christ Jesus."

Philippians 3:14 (KJV)

14 I press toward the mark for the prize of the high calling of God in Christ Jesus.

He is trying to get you into debt and into immoral relationships. He'll try any way he can to mess up your life.

You have a place of destiny which is fully released as you respond, build, and plant. How you respond; what you do or don't do with what God gives you can determine your destiny. Many wait and wait and never do anything with what God has given them. They want another prophetic word even though they never did anything with the Words they already received.

God does not change; however, He will adjust His decrees to fit our response. There are decrees and promises He has made that do not change, such as the covenant with Israel and His new covenant with us.

John 6:37-40 (KJV)

37 All that the Father giveth me shall come to me; and him that cometh to me I will in no wise cast out.

38 For I came down from heaven, not to do mine own will, but the will of him that sent me.

39 And this is the Father's will which hath sent me, that of all which he hath given me I should lose nothing, but should raise it up again at the last day.

40 And this is the will of him that sent me, that everyone which seeth the Son, and believeth on him, may have everlasting life: and I will raise him up at the last day.

John 6:44 (KJV)

44 No man can come to me, except the Father which hath sent me draw him: and I will raise him up at the last day.

There are others that He has adjusted, such as Abraham's plea for Sodom and Gomorrah and the sparing of Nineveh. God will adjust His responses to ours just as we adjust our responses to God's.

Genesis 18 (KJV)

18 And the Lord appeared unto him in the plains of Mamre: and he sat in the tent door in the heat of the day;

Understanding Heaven's Court System

2 And he lift up his eyes and looked, and, lo, three men stood by him: and when he saw them, he ran to meet them from the tent door, and bowed himself toward the ground,

3 And said, My Lord, if now I have found favour in thy sight, pass not away, I pray thee, from thy servant:

4 Let a little water, I pray you, be fetched, and wash your feet, and rest yourselves under the tree:

5 And I will fetch a morsel of bread, and comfort ye your hearts; after that ye shall pass on: for therefore are ye come to your servant. And they said, So do, as thou hast said.

6 And Abraham hastened into the tent unto Sarah, and said, Make ready quickly three measures of fine meal, knead it, and make cakes upon the hearth.

7 And Abraham ran unto the herd, and fetch a calf tender and good, and gave it unto a young man; and he hasted to dress it.

8 And he took butter, and milk, and the calf which he had dressed, and set it before them; and he stood by them under the tree, and they did eat.

9 And they said unto him, Where is Sarah thy wife? And he said, Behold, in the tent.

10 And he said, I will certainly return unto thee according to the time of life; and, lo, Sarah thy wife shall have a son. And Sarah heard it in the tent door, which was behind him.

11 Now Abraham and Sarah were old and well stricken in age; and it ceased to be with Sarah after the manner of women.

12 Therefore Sarah laughed within herself, saying, After I am waxed old shall I have pleasure, my lord being old also?

13 And the Lord said unto Abraham, Wherefore did Sarah laugh, saying, Shall I of a surety bear a child, which am old?

14 Is any thing too hard for the Lord? At the time appointed I will return unto thee, according to the time of life, and Sarah shall have a son.

15 Then Sarah denied, saying, I laughed not; for she was afraid. And he said, Nay; but thou didst laugh.

16 And the men rose up from thence, and looked toward Sodom: and Abraham went with them to bring them on the way.

17 And the Lord said, Shall I hide from Abraham that thing which I do;

18 Seeing that Abraham shall surely become a great and mighty nation, and all the nations of the earth shall be blessed in him?

19 For I know him, that he will command his children and his household after him, and they shall keep the way of the Lord, to do justice and judgment; that the Lord may bring upon Abraham that which he hath spoken of him.

Understanding Heaven's Court System

20 And the Lord said, Because the cry of Sodom and Gomorrah is great, and because their sin is very grievous;

21 I will go down now, and see whether they have done altogether according to the cry of it, which is come unto me; and if not, I will know.

22 And the men turned their faces from thence, and went toward Sodom: but Abraham stood yet before the Lord.

23 And Abraham drew near, and said, Wilt thou also destroy the righteous with the wicked?

24 Peradventure there be fifty righteous within the city: wilt thou also destroy and not spare the place for the fifty righteous that are therein?

25 That be far from thee to do after this manner, to slay the righteous with the wicked: and that the righteous should be as the wicked that be far from thee: Shall not the Judge of all the earth do right?

26 And the Lord said, If I find in Sodom fifty righteous within the city, then I will spare all the place for their sakes.

27 And Abraham answered and said, Behold now, I have taken upon me to speak unto the Lord, which am but dust and ashes:

28 Peradventure there shall lack five of the fifty righteous: wilt thou destroy all the city for lack of five? And he said, If I find there forty and five, I will not destroy it.

29 And he spake unto him yet again, and said, Peradventure there shall be forty found there. And he said, I will not do it for forty's sake.

30 And he said unto him, Oh let not the Lord be angry, and I will speak: Peradventure there shall thirty be found there. And he said, I will not do it, if I find thirty there.

31 And he said, Behold now, I have taken upon me to speak unto the Lord: Peradventure there shall be twenty found there. And he said, I will not destroy it for twenty's sake.

32 And he said, Oh let not the Lord be angry, and I will speak yet but this once: Peradventure ten shall be found there. And he said, I will not destroy it for ten's sake.

33 And the Lord went his way, as soon as he had left communing with Abraham: and Abraham returned unto his place.

Jonah 3 (KJV)

1 And the word of the Lord came unto Jonah the second time, saying,

2 Arise, go unto Nineveh, that great city, and preach unto it the preaching that I bid thee.

3 So Jonah arose, and went unto Nineveh, according to the word of the Lord. Now Nineveh was an exceeding great city of three days' journey.

Understanding Heaven's Court System

4 And Jonah began to enter into the city a day's journey, and he cried, and said, Yet forty days, and Nineveh shall be overthrown.

5 So the people of Nineveh believed God, and proclaimed a fast, and put on sackcloth, from the greatest of them even to the least of them.

6 For word came unto the king of Nineveh, and he arose from his throne, and he laid his robe from him, and covered him with sackcloth, and sat in ashes.

7 And he caused it to be proclaimed and published through Nineveh by the decree of the king and his nobles, saying, Let neither man nor beast, herd nor flock, taste any thing: let them not feed, nor drink water:

8 But let man and beast be covered with sackcloth, and cry mightily unto God: yea, let them turn every one from his evil way, and from the violence that is in their hands.

9 Who can tell if God will turn and repent, and turn away from his fierce anger that we perish not?

10 And God saw their works that they turned from their evil way; and God repented of the evil, that he had said that he would do unto them; and he did it not.

Abraham changed God's mind and so did Jonah. Remember Abraham. God said something like this: "Get out of my way Abraham; I'm coming down to destroy Sodom and Gomorrah." Then Abraham replied: "No way, God, if there is just fifty righteous... forty righteous... twenty righteous... how about ten righteous?" There is a place where you can barter with God, friends. What God said about you is not a guarantee.

Consider the life of Jonah. If it was true that what God says will happen and that we have nothing to do with it, then Jonah would have just rolled over and said, "Well, if God says He's coming down and bringing destruction and judgment to Nineveh, that's it, too bad for them. God said it so what can I do about it. God said it; it's got to happen!" Actually, Jonah ran from God because He knew that God would restrain His judgment if the people repented and Jonah didn't want that. Eventually, Jonah did deliver the word of God in Nineveh and the people repented. God did change His mind. Therefore, the Word must have been dependent on the actions of the people.

There are Princes of Persia in the spiritual realm working to prevent you from coming into the revelation and reality of your destiny. Something that God wanted to give you twenty-one days ago may be tied up. We need to release spiritual warfare and pray: "God, I ask for the angelic host to resist the enemy's assignments that are keeping back what you promised me in the area of my finances. Now, God, I ask that they would bring me my answer."

Understanding Heaven's Court System

Scripture tells us that we don't wrestle against flesh and blood, but demonic powers and principalities.

Ephesians 6:12 (KJV)

12 For we wrestle not against flesh and blood, but against principalities, against powers, against the rulers of the darkness of this world, against spiritual wickedness in high places.

Our spiritual eyes must be open so that we can see what is going on in the heavens. There is not a devil under every bush but there are more devils under bushes than many Christians are willing to admit. I'm not looking for demons. I don't have to look for them. They are there and I'm aware of them. I know that they want to destroy me but I'm neither afraid of them nor focused on them. I know who I am in Christ. This is for you to know who you are in Christ as well.

Know your authority and be vigilant. Even Mary understood this principle regarding prophetic words. After her prophetic word from the angel, she responded and prophetically decreed, *"Let it be to me according to your word."*

Luke 1:38 (KJV)

38 And Mary said, Behold the handmaid of the Lord; be it unto me according to thy word. And the angel departed from her.

She lined herself up with the Word from heaven, pulled it out of the spiritual realm into existence, and birthed it.

Chapter Six

Prophetic Decrees Have Power

Satan may have plans to disrupt God's plans and purposes but God has not given us a spirit of fear but of power and a sound mind based on the Word of God. There's no mistaking it, Satan has devised a plan of destruction against us. How often have we battled sickness, death, come up short, fought poverty, lack, desolation, or lost sight of our dreams or our divine destiny? However, God has already spoken victory concerning our circumstances. When we make a prophetic decree, we come into agreement with His Word.

God's Word says that what we decree becomes established, it becomes a foundation upon which to build, establish, and fulfill our destiny: *"Thou shalt also decree a thing, and it shall be established unto thee: and the light shall shine upon thy ways."*

Understanding Heaven's Court System

Job 22:28 (KJV)

28 Thou shalt also decree a thing, and it shall be established unto thee: and the light shall shine upon thy ways.

Prophetic decrees empower us to release power. Prophetic proclamations unlock and birth our destiny and the revelations, visions, and dreams God has given us. The power of God's Word through a prophetic decree will set the captive free, conquer sickness and disease, build and restore God's church, and release wealth and prosperity, spiritual and temporal abundance. We can reverse every decree the enemy has made concerning our lives by issuing a new decree. The devil says you can't, God says you can! The devil says you won't, God says you will! Proclaim what God says about you into the heavens. Take authority over things in the spirit that come against what God has already said about you, call out your miracles, and watch your destiny unfold.

Revelation 19:11-16 (KJV)

11 And I saw heaven opened, and behold a white horse; and he that sat upon him was called Faithful and True, and in righteousness he doth judge and make war.

12 His eyes were as a flame of fire, and on his head were many crowns; and he had a name written, that no man knew, but he himself.

13 And he was clothed with a vesture dipped in blood: and his name is called The Word of God.

14 And the armies which were in heaven followed him upon white horses, clothed in fine linen, white and clean.

15 And out of his mouth goeth a sharp sword, that with it he should smite the nations: and he shall rule them with a rod of iron: and he treadeth the winepress of the fierceness and wrath of Almighty God.

16 And he hath on his vesture and on his thigh a name written, King Of Kings, And Lord Of Lords.

First, I want you to see that the apostle John experienced this revelation when "heaven opened." It's evident that judgment and war happen there. This man, "Faithful and True", used the Word of God to wage this heavenly war: "And out of his mouth goes a sharp sword." That sharp sword is the Rhema word of God, heavenly revelation. In the same way, we must learn how to receive and employ God's Word and God's spoken revelation for our life, to judge and make war in the heavens. We also must learn to resist the forces of darkness that oppose our destiny so that we can bring His words to pass.

Understanding Heaven's Court System

We need to pray those prophetic words through- in the spirit and loose them in heaven so they'll be loosed on earth. The Bible speaks about calling forth those things that are not as though they already existed. Yes, God is before time.

Everything I have need of and everything that God wants me to do is in heaven! It's in heaven now. It's always been in heaven. It's in the eternal purposes of God. We just need to take our divine ATM debit card, insert it into the heavenly realm, and punch in the pin number. Whatever you ask for in prayer, believing, you shall receive it!

Mark 11:24 (KJV)

24 Therefore I say unto you, What things so ever ye desire, when ye pray, believe that ye receive them, and ye shall have them.

We need to make withdrawals from the resources of God to be what God has called us to be. God doesn't just drop it out of the heavenly realm in the sky though. We need to fast and pray for a while. Get out your ATM card, access heaven, and make a withdrawal.

Prophetic decrees are used for the sake of the kingdom to destroy works of the enemy or to release life to God's people. However, what we say or decree can also wreak havoc on innocent lives, including our own. They are bitter words spoken in secret about others or about oneself. They are negative words of gossip, slander, malice, or criticism. We need not allow ourselves to fall into these negative decrees.

Psalm 64:1-4 (KJV)

64 Hear my voice, O God, in my prayer: preserve my life from fear of the enemy.

2 Hide me from the secret counsel of the wicked; from the insurrection of the workers of iniquity:

3 Who whet their tongue like a sword, and bend their bows to shoot their arrows, even bitter words:

4 That they may shoot in secret at the perfect: suddenly do they shoot at him, and fear not.

Be careful what you say about people in secret or behind their backs because negative words are deadly. They slaughter the innocent, the blameless. Even words about yourself, like, "I can't do anything right" or, "I'm so stupid" open the doors for the enemy. In fact, demonic powers, the kingdom of darkness enforce negative and bitter words to destroy lives. It's no wonder Proverbs warns us that death and life are in the power of the tongue.

Understanding Heaven's Court System

Proverbs 18:21 (KJV)

21 Death and life are in the power of the tongue: and they that love it shall eat the fruit thereof.

Release decrees of life to bring healing, prosperity, and blessing into lives. Say good things about others, declare into the heavens what God says about them. God also wants you to speak out what He has said about you in His word or through prophetic promises to you.

Through prophetic decrees, we can speak things into existence as long as God has already promised those things in scripture or through a prophetic word. When we receive a word from God, we now have the authority to lay hold of it by faith. We can release the decrees of life by speaking about healing. By speaking over our body and speaking over others what the Bible says about miracles, we are activating the power of God's promises, we are enforcing things in heaven. The decrees of the Lord are words. God uses your decrees to deliver you from your adversary.

What has God said about you? Proclaim it into the heavens so the devil can hear and tremble. He's trying to keep you from your blessings! Take authority over anything that opposes your calling. What we do or don't do makes or breaks our prophetic word because everything we have need of originates in heaven. That's where our victory is! When we act, when we loose the Word and God's promises, we bring it to earth and into our lives, our homes, our ministries. What has God said about you, about your ministry, about your family, your business? Believe these truths and contend for them with your decrees, your words from your mouth.

Dictionaries describe a decree as an authoritative order having the force of law. It's a ruling, an announcement, a declaration, a verdict, a judgment, an order, or a pronouncement. It is to decide with authority and usually a legally binding command. Decrees are associated with authority and power. Decrees in the natural, occur all of the time, especially in government or in courts.

Let's look at some biblical decrees.

Jonah 3:5-7 (KJV)

5 So the people of Nineveh believed God, and proclaimed a fast, and put on sackcloth, from the greatest of them even to the least of them.

6 For word came unto the king of Nineveh, and he arose from his throne, and he laid his robe from him, and covered him with sackcloth, and sat in ashes.

7 And he caused it to be proclaimed and published through Nineveh by the decree of the king and his nobles, saying, Let neither man nor beast, herd nor

Understanding Heaven's Court System

flock, taste any thing: let them not feed, nor drink water:

Daniel 3:4 (KJV)

4 Then an herald cried aloud, To you it is commanded, O people, nations, and languages,

1 Samuel 11:7 (KJV)

7 And he took a yoke of oxen, and hewed them in pieces, and sent them throughout all the coasts of Israel by the hands of messengers, saying, Whosoever cometh not forth after Saul and after Samuel, so shall it be done unto his oxen. And the fear of the Lord fell on the people, and they came out with one consent.

Ezra 1:1 (KJV)

1 Now in the first year of Cyrus king of Persia, that the word of the Lord by the mouth of Jeremiah might be fulfilled, the Lord stirred up the spirit of Cyrus king of Persia, that he made a proclamation throughout all his kingdom, and put it also in writing, saying,

Ezra 6:1-2 (KJV)

Then Darius the king made a decree, and search was made in the house of the rolls, where the treasures were laid up in Babylon.

2 And there was found at Achmetha, in the palace that is in the province of the Medes, a roll, and therein was a record thus written:

Ezra 6:6-12 (KJV)

6 Now therefore, Tatnai, governor beyond the river, Shetharboznai, and your companions the Apharsachites, which are beyond the river, be ye far from thence:

7 Let the work of this house of God alone; let the governor of the Jews and the elders of the Jews build this house of God in his place.

8 Moreover I make a decree what ye shall do to the elders of these Jews for the building of this house of God: that of the king's goods, even of the tribute beyond the river, forthwith expenses be given unto these men, that they be not hindered.

9 And that which they have need of, both young bullocks, and rams, and lambs, for the burnt offerings of the God of heaven, wheat, salt, wine, and oil, according to the appointment of the priests which are at Jerusalem, let it be given them day by day without fail:

10 That they may offer sacrifices of sweet savors unto the God of heaven, and pray for the life of the king, and of his sons.

11 Also I have made a decree, that whosoever shall alter this word, let timber be pulled down from his house, and being set up, let him be hanged thereon; and let his house be made a dunghill for this.

Understanding Heaven's Court System

> *12 And the God that hath caused his name to dwell there destroy all kings and people that shall put to their hand to alter and to destroy this house of God which is at Jerusalem. I Darius have made a decree; let it be done with speed.*

Paraphrased: The king planned to release the money from his treasury so that the Jews, those returning from captivity, could rebuild the house of God. The King's message relayed this warning to anyone opposing or challenging his decree. "If anyone tries to alter this decree remember that I am King. My word carries weight! Whoever alters this decree shall be hung on the rafter of his house. Let his house be as a refuse heap and a dunghill. Let that happen to anyone who attempts to come against this decree." In ancient times, people would never defy the decree of a king because they would pay for their disobedience with their lives. Even today, there are consequences for breaking that which is decreed to be the law of the land.

Now, if natural decrees are that powerful, how much more powerful are spiritual decrees?

1 Peter 2:5 (KJV)

> *5 Ye also, as lively stones, are built up a spiritual house, a holy priesthood, to offer up spiritual sacrifices, acceptable to God by Jesus Christ.*

Bill Vincent

Revelation 1:4-6 (KJV)

4 John to the seven churches which are in Asia: Grace be unto you, and peace, from him which is, and which was, and which is to come; and from the seven Spirits which are before his throne;

5 And from Jesus Christ, who is the faithful witness, and the first begotten of the dead, and the prince of the kings of the earth. Unto him that loved us, and washed us from our sins in his own blood,

6 And hath made us kings and priests unto God and his Father; to him be glory and dominion for ever and ever. Amen.

In many societies, there is no higher calling than to be a priest or king. Yet, that is what God has called each of us as believers to be. "You also, as living stones, are being built up a spiritual house, a holy priesthood, to offer up spiritual sacrifices acceptable to God through Jesus Christ."

1 Peter 2:5 (KJV)

5 Ye also, as lively stones, are built up a spiritual house, an holy priesthood, to offer up spiritual sacrifices, acceptable to God by Jesus Christ.

We are as a kingdom of priests with Christ as High Priest and King of Kings overall. In Israel, priests and kings were divinely appointed, appointed by God, not elected or self-appointed. After being chosen, God delegated them with authority, with the power to act on His behalf for the good of the people. As believers, divinely appointed priests and kings of God's kingdom, delegated with His authority, what do you think happens when we actually decree into the spiritual realm and make known the manifold wisdom of God to demonic powers and principalities? The enemy cannot invade our house. The angelic hosts of heaven and Jesus Himself will back up our decrees, those that line up with His scriptural or revelatory words to us.

You have been given kingly anointing and authority; you've been made to sit in heavenly places.

Ephesians 2:6 (KJV)

6 And hath raised us up together, and made us sit together in heavenly places in Christ Jesus:

Every demon in hell trembles at your words when you know your position in Christ! They know that behind everything you say is the authority of heaven and Jesus Christ. The angels of God will come and arrest them. God releases angels to carry out His word in your life when you release the Word into heaven.

The enemy knows if you're unsure of your authority. If you are uncertain of whom you are in Christ, then get sure! Ask God for a revelation of who you are in Christ and receive that certainty that He, the hope of glory, lives in you.

John 1:12 (KJV)

12 But as many as received him, to them gave he power to become the sons of God, even to them that believe on his name:

John 15:15 (KJV)

15 Henceforth I call you not servants; for the servant knoweth not what his lord doeth: but I have called you friends; for all things that I have heard of my Father I have made known unto you.

Romans 5:1 (KJV)

5 Therefore being justified by faith, we have peace with God through our Lord Jesus Christ:

Romans 8:28 (KJV)

28 And we know that all things work together for good to them that love God, to them who are the called according to his purpose.

Understanding Heaven's Court System

Romans 8:31-39 (KJV)

31 What shall we then say to these things? If God be for us, who can be against us?

32 He that spared not his own Son, but delivered him up for us all, how shall he not with him also freely give us all things?

33 Who shall lay any thing to the charge of God's elect? It is God that justifieth.

34 Who is he that condemneth? It is Christ that died, yea rather, that is risen again, who is even at the right hand of God, who also maketh intercession for us.

35 Who shall separate us from the love of Christ? shall tribulation, or distress, or persecution, or famine, or nakedness, or peril, or sword?

36 As it is written, For thy sake we are killed all the day long; we are accounted as sheep for the slaughter.

37 Nay, in all these things we are more than conquerors through him that loved us.

38 For I am persuaded, that neither death, nor life, nor angels, nor principalities, nor powers, nor things present, nor things to come,

39 Nor height, nor depth, nor any other creature, shall be able to separate us from the love of God, which is in Christ Jesus our Lord.

1 Corinthians 6:17 (KJV)

17 But he that is joined unto the Lord is one spirit.

Ephesians 1:3-8 (KJV)

3 Blessed be the God and Father of our Lord Jesus Christ, who hath blessed us with all spiritual blessings in heavenly places in Christ:

4 According as he hath chosen us in him before the foundation of the world, that we should be holy and without blame before him in love:

5 Having predestinated us unto the adoption of children by Jesus Christ to himself, according to the good pleasure of his will,

6 To the praise of the glory of his grace, wherein he hath made us accepted in the beloved.

7 In whom we have redemption through his blood, the forgiveness of sins, according to the riches of his grace;

8 Wherein he hath abounded toward us in all wisdom and prudence;

Ephesians 2:10 (KJV)

10 For we are his workmanship, created in Christ Jesus unto good works, which God hath before ordained that we should walk in them.

Understanding Heaven's Court System

Ephesians 3:12 (KJV)

12 In whom we have boldness and access with confidence by the faith of him.

Colossians 1:13-14 (KJV)

13 Who hath delivered us from the power of darkness, and hath translated us into the kingdom of his dear Son:

14 In whom we have redemption through his blood, even the forgiveness of sins:

Colossians 2:9-10 (KJV)

9 For in him dwelleth all the fullness of the Godhead bodily.

10 And ye are complete in him, which is the head of all principality and power:

Hebrews 4:14-16 (KJV)

14 Seeing then that we have a great high priest, that is passed into the heavens, Jesus the Son of God, let us hold fast our profession.

15 For we have not an high priest which cannot be touched with the feeling of our infirmities; but was in all points tempted like as we are, yet without sin.

16 Let us therefore come boldly unto the throne of grace that we may obtain mercy, and find grace to help in time of need.

Philippians 4:3 (KJV)

3 And I entreat thee also, true yokefellow, help those women which labored with me in the gospel, with Clement also, and with other my fellow labourers, whose names are in the book of life.

Are you ready to release a few decrees into the heavenly realm? It's time to decree what God has promised you and what He has said about you. It's time to declare what the Bible and the prophetic words have said about you. You are going to make powerful prayers of proclamation of decree!

Isaiah 55:11 (KJV)

11 So shall my word be that goeth forth out of my mouth: it shall not return unto me void, but it shall accomplish that which I please, and it shall prosper in the thing whereto I sent it.

Start by reminding the devil about your destiny words from God. Speak all those prophetic words, visions, and revelations God has given you. Did God promise prosperity?

Take your decree and release it! Say, "Spirit of poverty, God has said I would prosper."

Understanding Heaven's Court System

3 John 2 (KJV)

2 Beloved, I wish above all things that thou mayest prosper and be in health, even as thy soul prospereth.

"His word is true and you will not hinder me." These are your words that you speak with priestly or kingly authority and the King of King's word backs you up! "My God, you promised me healing and prosperity. You listen to me devil of poverty, devil of sickness, you will not prevail!" Prophesy!

Romans 12:2 (KJV)

2 And be not conformed to this world: but be ye transformed by the renewing of your mind, that ye may prove what is that good, and acceptable, and perfect, will of God.

Release God's promises in your life for revival, miracles, health, and salvation for loved ones. Release decrees against opposing forces. Decree against religiosity! Decree against unbelief! Decree against apathy! "Father, I release revival!" Keep decreeing! Keep going, the heavens are opening. Grab another decree out of your quiver, "Father, I want miracles! You promised miracles." "Be healed in Jesus' name!" Then take authority against demons of infirmity, devils of sickness, every demon of disease. Keep going! Don't stop! The weapons of our warfare are mighty through God! Decree for your family and say, "God, I want my household saved! I want my entire household saved, Jesus! I take aim against the god of this world that has blinded their hearts and minds. Father, I release and prophesy the decree of the glorious Gospel of Truth, that it may pierce the hearts of those in my house." Now, for every person in your house you want to be saved, call them by name, and tell them to come out of darkness. Proclaim liberty to the captives. You are making known to demonic powers and principalities in the heavens your knowledge of the manifold wisdom of God.

Many fail to understand and apply the principle of spiritual aggression as they contend for their destiny.

Matthew 11:12 (KJV)

12 And from the days of John the Baptist until now the kingdom of heaven suffereth violence, and the violent take it by force.

The context of the Greek word used for violent in this passage isn't the same usage we apply it to today in the natural. Most violence today lands us in trouble! Rather, it describes a believer who is aggressive, zealous, and energetic in taking what has been made available to him or her. In this passage also, we are invited to seize the kingdom of God! This means that the kingdom isn't just going to "fall in our laps."

We have to covet, then take, or seize, or lay hold of the kingdom. The apostle Paul told the Corinthians to "covet earnestly the best gifts." Covet your promises and what God has said about you! People pressed in to touch the hem of Jesus' garments. They cried out in loud voices until He stopped by. They tore roofs off houses to get healing for a loved one. Release those decrees, take the kingdom of heaven by force! Be aggressive, be relentless.

God won't reprove you for raising the roof! He won't admonish you for your intensity! There's no limit on signs, wonders, and miracles! Just press in and lay hold of them. Be earnest, be zealous. Never be satisfied. Birth your destiny. Your decrees carry weight to activate all of God's promises. Keep doing this!

Chapter Seven

Break All the Way Through

We cannot move forward without breakthrough authority. We must rise up with a breakthrough that breaks all the way through. So many Christians get stuck in spiritual immaturity. Here are keys to helping you move to the next spiritual level.

You and I are living in a time of divine transition. Not only are things changing in the world around us, but people's lives are also changing too. Yes, God is shifting His people, perhaps even you, from one assignment to the next, from one sphere of influence or authority to the next, from one opportunity to the next, and from one season to the next. God is moving His people to the next level in our ministries or professional endeavors and in our personal lives. He is moving us forward in our destinies, advancing us in His purposes and equipping us for greater accomplishments than we have ever known. He is doing this so His kingdom

Understanding Heaven's Court System

can be established and increased in every sphere of every society on earth.

I believe that you are longing to fulfill God's great purposes for your life and that you desire to see His kingdom come and His will be done on earth, just as it is in heaven. If you are like many others, you may also be going through many changes in your life right now as God is preparing you to be used in new and different ways for His glory in the days ahead.

In the midst of transition, you may have many questions and moments of uncertainty. See the verse below concerning the times and seasons of our lives.

Daniel 2:21 (KJV)

21 And he changeth the times and the seasons: he removeth kings, and setteth up kings: he giveth wisdom unto the wise, and knowledge to them that know understanding:

Because God does give us wisdom and knowledge about the changes in our lives, you can be sure that you have everything you need to move to your next level. You have enough to make the shift. So wherever you are at this moment in your life, relax and say, "God, I want to go to my new level now. I am getting ready to move on and move up." Then follow these steps to help you through the transition process.

1st: Be convinced of the call. When God begins to take you through the process of change, you must make sure you are absolutely convinced of His call on your life and secure in His purposes as He has revealed them to you. When you know that God Himself has called you, nothing can convince you otherwise. You know that you have clearly perceived God's destiny for your life. You can hear the words resonating in your heart: "This is God's plan and purpose for me."

If you are not convinced of your call, if you waver or hesitate about it, then every time you hit a point of discouragement, an obstacle, or a difficulty, you will focus on your problems and give up. You will not overcome your challenges and pursue your destiny because your lack of conviction will lead you to abandon the mission to which God has called you. Only a deep conviction of your call will enable you to keep going when facing hardship. If you are going to deal with change effectively and persevere through difficulty, you must be so convinced of God's call on your life that you will not quit no matter what. This conviction will breed determination inside you and determination is essential to a successful transition.

2nd: Realize that a prophetic word is not enough. I like to receive prophetic words as much as anyone else does and I highly value the prophetic ministry. However, I do not change my address because of a prophetic word. I don't go to Africa the moment I receive a prophetic word. No, I have to hear God speak to my heart personally before I pack my boxes and move to a new address.

How should you respond when you receive a word from the Lord through prophecy? Let me offer some guidelines. Look for confirmation. Remember that a prophetic word should confirm what God is saying to you not determine it. For most prophecies, if a prophecy presents an entirely new thought or idea to you then receive the word but "hold" it until God sends some other confirmations that make its meaning clear to you. Don't wait too long. If God gives you confirmation after confirmation of a prophetic word and you do nothing with that clear direction then do not expect Him to continue "confirming" the word forever. No, after a while, His spirit will begin to slowly retreat from speaking to you. He may keep prompting you to act but after a while, you can become dull of hearing and miss moving on to the new level to which God has called you. Know the timing of God and move in it.

3rd: Consider how God has used you in the past. When you are moving on and moving up, God will build on your past experiences so make sure that you are positioned to allow your past to propel you into your future. See your past involvement and experiences, whether in ministry, in education, in social settings or in a professional capacity as training grounds. View those experiences as places where God has prepared you. When you consider the involvement and experience God has given you in the past, realize that He has been equipping you for the next level. God will expand you in those specific areas or build upon the foundation that is already in you. Even the seeming failures you have been through, the ones that bring disappointment and pain, are preparation rooms. Eventually, you will draw fresh water from the well of your experience and see that God has used your past to prepare you.

4th: Determine how you must change. When God begins to shift you from one assignment to another, you will go through a process of preparation. A great deal of preparation will have taken place through the experiences God has given you. But now, as you sense His leading you to the next level and begin to discern specifics about this new assignment, you will enter into a different kind of preparation. This preparation is not based on your past but must take place in the present. It involves the practical changes you need to make in your life in order to actually fulfill the new assignment or embrace the new season God has for you.

I want to make sure you know that moving to a new level in God or embracing a new assignment from Him is not only a spiritual exercise.

Understanding Heaven's Court System

Many times, people think they will be prepared for a new assignment if they pray more, worship more and read the Bible more regularly. These disciplines are important in times of transition, but there are also natural components to the changes God will bring in your life as He moves you forward. Moving to your new level will impact every area of your life so be equipped.

5th: Commit to overcoming the opposition. When God begins to move you to a new level, you will most likely encounter various forms of opposition. He moves you forward; the devil wants to move you backward or at least to cause you to stay where you are. He will orchestrate many thoughts or feelings designed to hold you back so let me encourage you. Go ahead and commit to overcoming any opposition that will come against you. Do not expect your transition to be easy. Know that the changes will have their challenges and make a proactive decision to emerge victorious, by God's grace, in every way.

One of the greatest barriers to moving forward to the next level is being too comfortable functioning where you are. You may want something different but when you move into it, you realize that the new assignment has no respect whatsoever for your comfort zone. It will stretch you, challenge you and be full of experiences that are unfamiliar to you. Choosing to stay in your comfort zone may mean that you never go to the next level in God. He will not force you to embrace anything new but I believe God wants you to do so in order to fulfill His purposes for your life. Any form of discomfort is worth overcoming in order to say yes to the next great thing God has for you.

6th: Be prepared for increased spiritual attacks. The more you move into God's unfolding purposes for your life, the more effective you become for Him and the more of a threat you become to the kingdom of darkness.

1 John 3:8 (KJV)

8 He that committeth sin is of the devil; for the devil sinneth from the beginning. For this purpose the Son of God was manifested, that he might destroy the works of the devil.

2 Corinthians 2:14 (KJV)

14 Now thanks be unto God, which always causeth us to triumph in Christ, and maketh manifest the savour of his knowledge by us in every place.

But our certain triumph does not eliminate the battle. We have an enemy; we are engaged in a spiritual war and we must fight. The attacks of our opposition seem to intensify when we move from one level to the next. Whenever we embrace a new season or take on a new assignment, warfare follows because the enemy wants to stop us from doing what we are called to do to advance God's kingdom. You are probably accustomed to the level of warfare you have experienced in your current circumstances but you need to know that when you step up, the battles will heat up. New battles require new strategies but your basic equipment remains the same. In Christ, you have spiritual armor to protect against the attacks of the enemy.

Ephesians 6:13-18 (KJV)

13 Wherefore take unto you the whole armour of God that ye may be able to withstand in the evil day, and having done all, to stand.

14 Stand therefore, having your loins girt about with truth, and having on the breastplate of righteousness;

15 And your feet shod with the preparation of the gospel of peace;

16 Above all, taking the shield of faith, wherewith ye shall be able to quench all the fiery darts of the wicked.

17 And take the helmet of salvation, and the sword of the Spirit, which is the word of God:

18 Praying always with all prayer and supplication in the Spirit, and watching thereunto with all perseverance and supplication for all saints;

You also have the weapon of His Word, the power of His Spirit and the reinforcement of other believers. Use everything available to you as a Christian and though attacks will come, you will overcome with God's help.

7th: Accept acceptance. Once you are convinced that God has called you to the next level and you truly step into it, you will begin to feel the responsibility and authority of that level. You will sense an anointing and a grace from God to do what you are supposed to be doing in your new season. As you are settling into your new place, you must resist the temptation to be shy, sheepish or apologetic about what God has done in you. Be gracious, of course, but do not let false humility creep into your thoughts or conversation.

A genuinely humble person accepts and acknowledges what God has done in his or her life. If you want to live in true humility, do not try to explain away God's work in your life. Instead, be honest about what He is doing, admit your need for His grace and give Him glory without being religious.

God calls and anoints certain people for certain roles and tasks according to His wisdom and grace. When the time comes for Him to move you to a new level, be aware that you are now released; you can now flow in the Lord without the former limitations. As you simply trust His wisdom and follow His lead, your confidence and anointing will continue to increase. Do not become proud, but neither should you deny who God has designed you to be.

8th: Remember that transition takes time. Successful transition does not happen quickly, and for you, getting to the next level may take time. I want to encourage you now to determine to be patient as you move into your new season. Do not try to change things for yourself too quickly or rush ahead of God's timing. God has designed change to be a process, not an event. He is certainly interested in the end result of the changes He orchestrates in our lives but the process of growth and maturity that accompanies change is also very important to Him. For this reason, He typically works diligently, deliberately and more slowly than you might want! But you need to remember that His timing is perfect; it is part of a grand plan for your life and it will bring you great joy and fulfillment as you patiently cooperate with it.

Like the Israelites, you are on a journey toward the full possession of His promises to you and you will face opposition as you go. But God has the same strategy for victory in your life as He had for His people centuries ago: little by little. You will get where He wants you to go one step at a time, one day at a time, one victory at a time.

9th: Move ahead with bold faith. Any time God is shifting you from one level to the next, there comes a point at which you simply must "go for it." This is a point beyond commitment, a point past making a firm decision to move forward; it is the point at which you actually put one foot in front of the other and take the critical steps that will solidify you in your new position. This is the point at which faith springs into action and becomes more alive than ever before. God's way is a way of faith. You can know all kinds of concepts and principles but without faith, bold faith, you will never step out to achieve all God has purposed for you.

Jesus is saying to you, "Come on! Take that step of bold faith. I am ready and waiting to walk with you." Always remember, God is faithful. He is faithful to finish the work He has begun in you.

Philippians 1:6 (KJV)

6 Being confident of this very thing, that he which hath begun a good work in you will perform it until the day of Jesus Christ:

Move on and move up. I'll meet you at your next level! Break all the way through.

Bill Vincent

Chapter Eight
Reassignments Coming

This is a bonus chapter because it was added after the first draft was complete. I heard God speak to me about promotion and reassignments and it was perfect for the tail of the book. Please note that God wants us all to attain new heights of reassignments coming. The Lord spoke to me that there would be some radical adjustments and changes coming for us all.

There have been some changes in many people's callings. New assignments were released from the heavenly adjustment department. This will be the start of some major realignments and reassignments coming. Many people have been experiencing serious levels of discouragement and warfare. I have been praying daily for a breakthrough about this for myself and for others.

God spoke to me that my case in Heaven had been reviewed and an adjustment offer had been released. I have never heard this before and it took me by surprise. I also heard that this was happening to many people right now. God then spoke about new offers being given to everyone. I was told by God that after reviewing my ministry, I was being offered a choice. I could continue in the current position that I occupy in the Kingdom of God, or I could take a special assignment that would produce more results in the Kingdom with regard to the upcoming revival. For years I have been a "Courts of Heaven Reporter." But this changed recently when I was promoted to a "Courts of Heaven Prophet" which comes with a lot of interaction in the heavenly realm and being part of counsel meetings similar to what is described in Zechariah 3. It also brings extreme levels of spiritual warfare. Something changed for me again just recently. I knew that if I took this new assignment then the supernatural encounters that I have been having daily would reduce dramatically. I would still be a prophet, but my assignment and position would change. I knew that what appears to be a demotion on Earth is indeed a promotion in God's eyes.

1 Peter 5:6 (KJV)

6 Humble yourselves therefore under the mighty hand of God, that he may exalt you in due time:

Jesus took a major demotion when He left His place of glory and came to Earth to save us all. He will promote the humble and the Lord is saying over and over right now that "due time is overdue." There is a backlog of repayment and unanswered prayers coming to many people.

I was given a choice and the Lord said He would bless me either way. I chose the new assignment which is actually an upgraded version of my original calling. When we make decisions that will help grow the kingdom, we will be blessed.

I want to try to explain my promotion the best I can. Let me say this, the availability of this promotion is for more than just me. When I learned to operate and submit things to the courts of heaven, anything that I saw as an injustice, I could submit to the courts of heaven. I thought this level was an amazing level.

The promotion was this. I would no longer be as a plaintiff submitting my case or injustice to the courts. I would now be one of the judges. God says that we are to sit with Him in heavenly places. I would not be the only and final judge but I would be co-laboring with God and this is according to the Word of God. I would be able to make judgments that God the ultimate judge would be in agreement with. If I made judgments, they would have to line up to the Word of God. This does not give me access to judging things with wrong heart or motives. I have to be in agreement with God the ultimate judge and only do as I see the Father do. Because of this promotion, instead of pleading my case, I am able to submit on behalf of my family justice. I can decree that any prophetic promises that have been hindered or held back are to be released according the Word of the Lord. This is something I am living out as I write this chapter. I am learning as I go and taking it one step at a time. I first dealt with injustices. My family and I should be blessed, healed, set free and delivered. I also dealt with the promises to our ministry and revival all across the land. Then, I began to deal with all the promises concerning our country and even released decrees for the 2016 presidential election.

Matthew 19:29 (KJV)

29 And every one that hath forsaken houses, or brethren, or sisters, or father, or mother, or wife, or children, or lands, for my name's sake, shall receive an hundredfold, and shall inherit everlasting life.

God has hidden many people away in prison- like Joseph in Genesis 41. Joseph was released suddenly and repaid for all his pain and suffering. The prison was not a fun place to be but it was a place of hope and safety to him as he waited for the fulfillment of the dreams God had given to him as a child (Genesis 37). God spoke to me that He is beginning to call forth the prisoners of hope.

Zechariah 9:12 (KJV)

12 Turn you to the strong hold, ye prisoners of hope: even today do I declare that I will render double unto thee;

This is a time to press into the Lord in prayer and get ready for your marching orders that will come. God is going to start releasing the prisoners of hope. He is going to bring new hope and use you to bring hope to people in need of His love.

So get your hopes up because you are going to be repaid double for all your trouble.

God is giving strategic seasons of dreams. By the time this book is released, it will mark the release of strategic dreams from God. Watch for dreams and night visitations as higher-level revelation is going to start pouring out to you. In some cases, you might not remember these types of dreams or visitations. The reason for this is that God is going to reveal it to you in a way that will hide it from the enemy.

Daniel 2:19-22 (KJV)

19 Then was the secret revealed unto Daniel in a night vision. Then Daniel blessed the God of heaven.

Understanding Heaven's Court System

20 Daniel answered and said, Blessed be the name of God for ever and ever: for wisdom and might are his:

21 And he changeth the times and the seasons: he removeth kings, and setteth up kings: he giveth wisdom unto the wise, and knowledge to them that know understanding:

22 He revealeth the deep and secret things: he knoweth what is in the darkness, and the light dwelleth with him.

God is releasing wisdom and power and concealing strategies and revelation. This will help hide your promotion and plans from the enemy and bring you less warfare. Times and seasons are changing quickly so be aware that the way you currently do things might not work in the new season that is upon us now. The Lord is releasing deep and hidden things over the next month. He is going to reveal the plans of the enemy against you and bring them into the light. Watch for a change in affiliations and locations to start unfolding.

Get ready for things to start happening much more quickly! Get ready for deeper dreams and for your marching orders to come.

The enemy is trying to forge his own marches, assemblies, and protests but they are part of a spiritual way that is stirring the great need to go to court in heaven and plead our case.

About the Author

Bill Vincent is no stranger to understanding the power of God. Not only has he spent over twenty years as a Minister with a strong prophetic anointing, he is now also an apostle and author with Revival Waves of Glory Ministries in Litchfield, IL. Along with his wife, Tabitha, he leads a team providing apostolic oversight in all aspects of ministry, including service, personal ministry, and Godly character.

Bill offers a wide range of writings and teachings from deliverance to experiencing the presence of God and developing apostolic cutting edge church structure. Drawing on the power of the Holy Spirit through years of experience in Revival, Spiritual Sensitivity, and Deliverance Ministry, Bill now focuses mainly on pursuing the presence of God and breaking the power of the devil off of people's lives.

His books, 49 and counting, have since helped many people to overcome the spirits and curses of

Understanding Heaven's Court System

Satan. For more information or to keep up with Bill's latest releases, please visit www.revivalwavesofgloryministries.com.

To contact Bill, feel free to follow him on twitter @revivalwaves.

Recommended Books

By Bill Vincent

Overcoming Obstacles

Glory: Pursuing God's Presence

Defeating the Demonic Realm

Increasing Your Prophetic Gift

Increase Your Anointing

Keys to Receiving Your Miracle

The Supernatural Realm

Waves of Revival

Increase of Revelation and Restoration

The Resurrection Power of God

Discerning Your Call of God

Apostolic Breakthrough

Glory: Increasing God's Presence

Love is Waiting – Don't Let Love Pass You By

The Healing Power of God

Glory: Expanding God's Presence

Receiving Personal Prophecy
Signs and Wonders
Signs and Wonders Revelations
Children Stories
The Rapture
The Secret Place of God's Power
Building a Prototype Church
Breakthrough of Spiritual Strongholds
Glory: Revival Presence of God
Overcoming the Power of Lust
Glory: Kingdom Presence of God
Transitioning to the Prototype Church
The Stronghold of Jezebel
Healing After Divorce
A Closer Relationship With God
Cover Up and Save Yourself
Desperate for God's Presence
The War for Spiritual Battles
Spiritual Leadership
Global Warning
Millions of Churches

Destroying the Jezebel Spirit

Awakening of Miracles

Deception and Consequences Revealed

Are You a Follower of Christ

Don't Let the Enemy Steal from You!

A Godly Shaking

The Unsearchable Riches of Christ

Heaven's Court System

Satan's Open Doors

Armed for Battle

The Wrestler

Spiritual Warfare: Complete Collection

Growing In the Prophetic

Faith

The Angry Fighter's Story

Understanding Heaven's Court System

Restoration of the Soul

Web Site:

www.revivalwavesofgloryministries.com

www.ingramcontent.com/pod-product-compliance
Lightning Source LLC
Chambersburg PA
CBHW070144080526
44586CB00015B/1841